Letters to the Sons of Society

Letters to the

Sons of Society

A Father's Invitation to Love, Honesty, and Freedom

Shaka Senghor

Convergent · New York

Published in the United States by Convergent Books, an
imprint of Random House, a division of Penguin Random
House LLC, New York.

CONVERGENT BOOKS is a registered trademark and its C
colophon is a trademark of Penguin Random House LLC.

Library of Congress Cataloging-in-Publication Data
Names: Senghor, Shaka, author.
Title: Letters to the sons of society / Shaka Senghor.
Description: First edition. | New York: Convergent, [2021]
Identifiers: LCCN 2021040092 (print) | LCCN 2021040093
(ebook) | ISBN 9780593238011 (hardcover) |
ISBN 9780593238028 (ebook)
Subjects: LCSH: Fathers and sons—United States. | African
American boys—Psychology. | Children of prisoners—
United States. | African American fathers—United States.
Classification: LCC HQ755.85 .S466 2021 (print) |
LCC HQ755.85 (ebook) | DDC 306.874/20896073—dc23
LC record available at https://lccn.loc.gov/2021040092
LC ebook record available at https://lccn.loc.gov/2021040093

Printed in Canada on acid-free paper

crownpublishing.com

2 4 6 8 9 7 5 3 1

First Edition

Frontispiece: courtesy of the author
Design by Fritz Metsch

This book is dedicated to the sons
and daughters of society

In memoriam of my brother Sherrod Redd

Your children are not your children.

They are the sons and daughters of Life's longing for itself.

They come through you but not from you,

And though they are with you yet they belong not to you.

—KAHLIL GIBRAN

Contents

Introduction   xi

A Trip to the Gas Station   3

Love Is Unconditional   17

Racism   27

The Hoop in the Driveway   41

Freedom Is My Legacy   49

Freedom Is Writing Your Own Narrative   59

Parenting   75

Stop Resisting   85

Isolation   97

Decision Making   111

The Freedom to Cry   117

Death Row Sons   129

The Ford Taurus   141

Addiction   151

Dear Jay, Dear Kalief   165

Love Is Never Abuse   175

American Beauty   187

Joy Day   205

To the Sons of Society   209

Acknowledgments   215

Introduction

It was an early-spring day in Detroit, and I was riding in the passenger seat of my dad's car, scared to death. We were en route to his aunt's house, where a huge Great Dane waited for me in the backyard. I was thirteen at the time and comfortable around most dogs, but that beast was another thing altogether. It would scarf down pounds of food out of a five-gallon bucket, and still seemed hungry. I figured he could eat me whole.

Fortunately, when we got to my great-aunt's house, all thoughts of going out into the yard ended when I realized that it was game two of the 1986 Eastern Conference playoff finals: the Boston Celtics versus the Chicago Bulls, Larry Bird versus Michael Jordan. For a thirteen-year-old basketball nut, it was nirvana.

The game itself was one thing. Jordan, all swagger, his wristband pulled up to his forearm, the way he looked over his shoulder at the basket as he jogged back on defense—he dropped 63 points on the Celtics, and still the Bulls lost. But what really caught my eye, and what caused me excitement and agony in equal measure, was those shoes: those red, white, and black Air Jordans.

Excitement because surely that was where Jordan's magic resided, right? I mean, a pair of Jordans would give any player extra lift, extra power, extra speed. But agony, too, because of what had happened to me a year earlier.

In April 1985, as my seventh-grade year was winding down, the first Air Jordans dropped—but it was also the time when my parents were preparing to separate for the second time. They told me I was going to live with my dad and my uncle Charles on Yacama Road, on the east side of Detroit. Once there, I was fortunate enough to make friends quickly, and as the summer came around, I found my place among the boys on the block. It was a dope summer. We hung out, rode our bikes, played ball—we didn't have a care in the world. But there were clouds forming. Come late August, I would be heading to a new school in a new neighborhood. The boys on Yacama Road regaled me all summer with tales of the fights they'd had while walking to school, the guys from the surrounding neighborhoods of 7 Mile Road or 8 Mile Road picking on them. I should be ready, I was told, to defend our hood.

The only thing that got me through the fear was a back-to-school shopping trip my father had promised me. I wanted one thing: a new pair of Air Jordans. They cost twice as much as any pair of shoes I had ever owned, but my heart was set on a pair. My dad didn't seem to get my hints—instead of heading to the Eastland Center, where I knew there were some Air Jordans at the Foot Locker, he drove us to JCPenney in Highland Park. There were no Air Jordans there. Instead, he made me try on a pair of canvas Air Force 1s, and when they fit, he bought them, and we trudged back to the car. I was devastated.

I wasn't devastated for long; about a week before school started, he arrived home one day with a Foot Locker bag. Inside, sure enough, was a pair of Air Jordans. Though they weren't the exact ones I'd wanted (seriously, thirteen-year-olds!), I was still ecstatic and couldn't wait to stride into Nolan Middle School with my Jordans on my feet. With the benefit of age, I realize now that my father was doing his best to bring me joy during a difficult time in our lives. For a kid like me, often moving around and being forced to make new friends, having cool sneakers was like having the golden key to the club of adolescent acceptance.

But my joy didn't last long. I decided that the Jordans were less a fashion statement than a practical pair of shoes that would turn me into their namesake on the court. In my first gym class, I got a quick steal, ran off down the court like a cheetah, and shot a jumper that swished through the rim, barely touching the net. I felt faster, quicker, and more athletic than anyone else on the court. It was true, the shoes were magic—but the damage was done. At the end of the class there was a large crease across the toe that could never be undone and scuff marks all over the sneakers. I had broken the cardinal rule of sneaker ownership: They were not, in fact, athletic shoes. They were to be worn for style and style only. Since I knew that there was no way of resurrecting the shoes to their pristine glory, I doubled down: I continued to play basketball in them both at school and at home.

One day, after I came inside from playing, my dad looked

down at the shoes and asked me if they were the same Air Jordans that he had just spent his hard-earned money on. The shame hit me; I lowered my head and mumbled yes; he shook his head and walked away. He didn't yell at me or tell me to go to my room. It was worse: I could sense his disappointment, and for days afterward he barely spoke to me.

He finally broke the silence one day when I got back from school. "I got you a pair of gym shoes," he said. "They're in your bedroom." Imagine my horror at finding a Payless bag on my bed and inside a pair of Pro Wing high-top knock-off Jordans. Instead of soft, high-quality leather, they were made of hard, cheap plastic. The soles were plastic, too, guaranteed to make me slide all over the gym floor. I raced down the hallway in tears and told my dad that I would never wear those shoes. He just said, "Until you become more responsible and take care of the things I provide that's all you're going to get."

That was the beginning of a protracted war of wills between us. I tossed the shoes into the closet, and for the rest of the school year I wore a mixture of older sneakers and the Jordans because he refused to buy me anything else and I was *not* wearing the Pro Wings.

Later that summer, my dad, my uncle, my cousin, two younger sisters, and I went to visit my grandfather in Mississippi. Dad forced me to take the Pro Wings, telling me in no uncertain terms that those were the shoes I'd be wearing; I also thought to pack a pair of beaten-up Nikes. After two sweltering weeks in the mosquito-infested heat of Mississippi, my dad returned to Detroit, leaving us to stay down in the country with our grandfather for a few more weeks. When I got back to Detroit, my dad noticed that I was wearing the

Nikes and asked me where the Pro Wings were. I feigned shock and said I'd I accidentally left them down in Mississippi.

I think I caught him stifling a laugh at that obvious lie. I realize now that he was desperate to teach me the value of things, while I just wanted to fill the void of my broken home life with the approval of friends. Somewhere in between was where our love lay.

The next few years were traumatic for me, and I would eventually go to prison at the age of nineteen. It wouldn't be until years later that my dad and I worked to unpack all of the things that had led up to my incarceration, and we did so through the letters we exchanged during the nearly two decades I was in prison. From the moment I was taken to the county jail up until my release, my dad and I wrote hundreds of letters back and forth, discussing the challenges of fatherhood, what it means to be a son and a man, the difficulties and joys of being Black in America, of learning to heal and be emotionally present to one another.

The harrowing ordeal faced by the fathers of incarcerated people is a story seldom told. On September 13, 1994, my dad wrote, "For me waking up each day and not being able to call you or just see you once in a while is very painful. Sometimes I just sit and cry because I miss you so much." Yet in those letters, he loved on me, debated with me, challenged me, and explained his life to me; in turn, I sent him love and answered his challenges and tried to make sense of my own life. His words gave me a source of protection and love and the building blocks of manhood when I needed them most, in those pain-filled, traumatic years of my incarceration. The level of intimacy generated by those letters is something I'm

coming to fully understand only now as I approach my fifties.
I am incredibly lucky to have a father so open to love and to
honesty, and it's these two attributes I've tried to pay forward
to my own sons in this book.

I believe that letters are one of the most intimate forms
of communication. They give us an insight into the most
frightening, uncertain places and can serve as an introduction to what it means to be passionate, to love, to dream, to
settle differences. I devoured books of letters in prison and
continue to be inspired by them: those by W.E.B. Du Bois;
Martin Luther King, Jr.'s "Letter from Birmingham Jail"; the
letters of George Jackson; Nelson Mandela's prison letters; the
letters of James Baldwin, Maya Angelou, Alice Walker, Toni
Morrison, and Ta-Nehisi Coates. Across the centuries, letters
have served to challenge ideas, create movements, highlight
contradictions, and inspire love.

And they have always tended to reveal the deepest feelings
of their writer. I remember one I sent to my dad from solitary,
in which I urged him to move on with his life because I felt
I'd never get out of prison. His answer was a simple one: "I'll
never leave your side." Those words kept me alive. The pile
of his letters that now sits in my office here in my house in
Los Angeles is a testament to his always being there no matter what was happening in my life. Each envelope with my
name and prison number etched in my dad's writing moved
me closer to my destination as a father.

I am the proud father of two sons, Jay and Sekou. Jay lives
in Detroit; he was born in 1992, while I was incarcerated.
Sekou is nine years old. He lives in Los Angeles, half the time
with his mother and half the time with me. My sons are the

hope of the world. I see in them so many things that I was not at their age—they embody hope and joy and love.

I've written this book with the intent of doing for them what my father did for me all those years ago: filling them in on my life, on my dreams for them, and on what I wish I'd gotten right through the years. But I also hope to reach boys and young men across America and their parents, especially their fathers. For so long, the voice of fathers has been limited to discipline and toughness; rarely do we get to speak honestly about our own fears and mistakes or explore the deeper, softer emotions that are crucial to effective fatherhood. So when I speak to my sons, I'm speaking not just to them but to sons everywhere and to their fathers. Without sharing our deepest emotions, we will remain unable to fully connect or talk out the pain into a place of love.

The basis of all these letters is love. They are an invitation to love more passionately, more completely, and more truly than ever before. Only with that love can we find a way out of the violence, hardship, and sense of dread so many of us have experienced. My prayer is that this book of letters might reach all the sons of society and start important conversations about how we can improve our world so that children can face the future with hope and excitement, filled with a sense that they are truly valued and deeply loved.

Los Angeles, California
February 2021

Letters to the Sons of Society

A Trip to the Gas Station

Dear Jay,

Being able to call someone your son or daughter is one of the greatest privileges known to humankind. The responsibility is profound: children don't choose to be brought onto this spinning planet, and though we hope that each new life comes from a place of love and care, too often a child is a by-product of carelessness or selfishness. You don't get to choose your parents, your moment of birth, or even something as simple and important as your name. These are privileges a parent should carry out with care and compassion; it's not a light and airy thing, being a parent. Or at least it shouldn't be.

So here, Jay, I call you "son," "my son." But too often I feel like a fraud when I use this word to describe you. I feel like a fraud because I have not been a good father. I have not worn the mantle of being your parent with due care. I have not lived up to the privilege of your existence. I have not walked beside you in the ways I know you have needed.

In fact—and it devastates me to say this—there are days when I don't feel like your father at all. Those words burn a hole in me, and I wish I would never even bring them to mind, much less write them. But I have done so, and I must bear the weight of those words here, now, forever.

Some days I'm convinced that we were closer when I was in prison, but prison has a way of skewing all things—the brutality all around you, the sense that your humanity is somehow on hold or contingent upon others. I now realize that the memory of our being closer while I was inside was one of the illusions I had about being a father. I thought the letters we exchanged, the irregular visits, and the few yearly phone calls were solid enough bridges to keep us connected until I was released. But what were they really, compared to the days—years' worth of them—when I was absent?

Have you ever seen the film of the Tacoma Narrows Bridge? It was a suspension bridge up in Washington State that couldn't handle the wind. It swayed often and eventually buckled and fell into the Puget Sound. That was what it was like to base my hopes for us on those letters, calls, and visits: eventually, things were going to collapse under the pressure of the air. I now realize how wrong I was, how impossible it is to forge bonds of familiarity under the oppressive weight of a prison sentence. I was so bent on trying to connect with you and guide you down a different path that I didn't stop to think about the path you were forging on your own on the other side of the bars. How could I have done so? Being a parent is complicated, in or out of prison. But in prison? Impossible, perhaps.

Add to all this, as it must always be added: you were a

Black boy. Childhood for anyone is a burden. (I have no idea where the idea that childhood should be carefree comes from.) And being a Black child is harder. We are burdened with a lack of overt affection, and we are not invited to try out the world as innocents. From the start, the world treats us like little men and women; we are told to suck it up, to be tough, that emotion is weakness, that the cold world is coming for us so we'd better be ready. Still, you were so innocent once—a little boy I wanted to protect from all the terrible things that young Black boys face. So many terrible things, things that an innocent child couldn't conceive of—was I supposed to tell you all of them so that you could avoid them? Was I supposed to hide you from them like Moses in the rushes? Which way should a parent of a Black child turn? To honesty or to obfuscation?

These thoughts swirl around in my mind still. They're like monsters just beyond the edge of the yard, moaning and keening on a humid summer night, there in the black trees. I try to ignore them, but every night they're there.

I wanted so hard to be a good father to you, Jay, but here in the calm of my yard in Los Angeles, with the monsters whimpering from the dark streets beyond the fence, I find myself thinking back to the beginning and imagining all the things I wish I could have given you when you needed me the most.

Our first visit was at the Michigan Reformatory in Ionia, Michigan. It was the fall of 1993; you were twenty-one months old. I had never met you, never held you, never been woken in the small hours to save you from nightmares. To that point in your life I had only ever seen photos of you, the ones that your grandfather sent along with his letters. My father would fill me in on your personality and write that you reminded him so much of me. That must have been so painful for him, me incarcerated and his grandson reminding him with every coo and first word that his own son was gone. But I took great comfort from those letters, because I knew my father was doing his best to take care of you, to create a connection between his son and his grandson, even though we were miles apart and separated by the mandate of the state.

Imagine, then, the day that my name was called: I had a visitor. I was shocked. It had been so long since someone had come to see me; so long, in fact, that I had blocked out the expectation of seeing anyone. That was how I coped; I low blocked any thoughts of family or affection or connection with the outside world. I was like a tackle aiming for the knees, bringing down any hope so that it couldn't get past me, couldn't hurt me, couldn't make my prison life any more depressing than it already was.

So imagine again: As I reached the visiting room, my hands began to shake, and there were great bolts of sweat dripping down my sides. Here was hope, getting by my defenses, causing me to tremble and sway like a poorly built bridge. The hope was this: I was finally going to see the son I had heard so much about. And there you were, just twenty-one months old, a beautiful brown ball of curiosity and energy. I watched my dad carry you in, and it reminded me of the way he would carry my sisters and put them to bed.

But my excitement at seeing you soon turned to heartbreak when I reached your way and you wouldn't allow me to pick you up. I had created a narrative about our close bond, but your reality was that I hadn't been in your life and you had no clue who I was. I had missed all of the bonding moments that take place between children and their fathers. I hadn't wiped away your tears, hadn't held a bottle to your lips in the middle of the night, hadn't changed your diaper. All I had been was a name, the word "father" without the meaning behind it.

I had been a ghost.

You didn't want me, and I was crushed. When I tried holding you, you cried so hard, and the echo of that cry haunted me for days after our visit. Your tears woke me up out of my sleep, clawing at me, monsters each one—no longer beyond the trees but now in my cell, ripping at my sanity. "He will grow up seeing you as the bogeyman," my mind said, "or even worse, the invisible man." Those thoughts took the blood out of my body, left me weak.

For days, I was of no use. I would lie on my bunk, held down by the gravity of those thoughts. It was the weight of realizing that I hadn't been there for you, that I had forfeited my right to be your father. Each time my cell door slammed, I stewed in the knowledge of my failure, of how wrong it was to call you "son," and how much I longed to do so.

The Michigan Reformatory is nearly three hours from Detroit. Your grandfather couldn't afford to bring you as often as he would have liked or as often as I wanted. Even when you came, the rules were so restrictive that they made it almost impossible to bond organically. I couldn't sit you on my lap or tousle your hair. These simple things, these simple acts of affection and love, are available to other fathers and sons everywhere except here. And it was clear that you were in pain, too. You couldn't take me home with you, away from that place, and you cried every time you had to leave.

As you got older, I realized that I would have to make you grow up fast, faster than children in less trying circumstances. (Now I realize that this isn't only what happens to the children of incarcerated parents; being a child generally ends early for Black boys.) I had made choices; because of those choices, I had saddled you with a great daily burden. All parents do this to some degree—remember, no child chooses to be born—but I had added to this cosmic truth a layer of pain from my decisions, the ones that had led me to this prison. Now, every time I saw you, I had to remind you that you couldn't touch my hair or rub my beard—rules designed to "protect children" when really, they just added pain upon pain. Those of us in prison had no power to change those rules; our children had to see us shorn of all agency. It was a perversion of the norm; parents protect their children from feeling helpless, but not in prison. There the parent is without power, and the child sees. On some visits you just sat across from me and stared. I would ask you what you were thinking, and you always said, "Nothing, Daddy." But I knew there was something—the tears that glistened at the corner of your eyes revealed that something, a thing so powerful, so damaging, that I was grateful you were unable to put it into words. You sensed that, I think, and held back. But the something was this: Because of my choices, you were locked up, too. Your innocence was held hostage right alongside mine.

For nineteen years I tried to be a father to you, to ensure that we stayed connected and you knew you were loved. I owed you a father, and I did what I could to give you what you deserved. But it was never enough; it could never be enough.

Jay, I thought about you every day in there. I would lie on my bunk wondering what your life was like on the outside. I imagined you playing ball and running through the neighborhood like other kids. I pictured you going to amusement parks and going to prom and all the things that make up a childhood. I so desperately wanted for you to be free to be a child, to maintain the innocence of boyhood, even though I sensed at the edge of my vision that your maintaining your innocence was impossible. So many young men from our family had walked the pathway of gun violence and prison sentences. I wanted you to break that chain, break that cycle, and live a truly innocent life.

And then I was out.

I brought many things home with me; one of them was the story I had created about who we were, a story filled with hope and optimism. Some of my friends had returned to build beautiful relationships with their children, and it gave me hope. When I went home, I would teach you all the things I knew and learn all that you knew. We would ride off into the sunset, father and son together.

You were eighteen when I walked out of prison and had every right to decide whether I was going to be a part of your life. But me? I wasn't prepared for anything other than that dreamlike vision of my homecoming. I thought my role was to save you from all the things that destroy Black boys and men, all the things that had destroyed me. So I engaged you in the ways I engaged the other young men I mentored. I made suggestions on how you should dress; pressed you to fill out job applications; challenged you to read books; urged you to avoid hanging around with the wrong crowd; and above all pushed you to chase a dream for yourself, a dream I didn't even know if you had.

I showed up as a mentor, not a father. You needed a father. That was my blindness, the blurry vision of a man newly born into freedom. I'm truly sorry that I didn't possess the wisdom or thoughtfulness to figure out what you wanted or needed from me.

What did I find of you when I got home? There were whispers through the family that you had smoked weed laced with something. Whatever the cause, it was devastating to watch you battle what I perceived as your demons. I was frustrated not knowing what was true—how could I? I had been gone all your life. Faced with the possibility that you had serious issues to address, I lacked the emotional maturity and insight to know what to do about it.

In addition, I knew that you were struggling with getting to know me as a person. I didn't make things easy, because I overcompensated for not having been there. I thought that buying you things and sharing the little bit of money I had would show you how committed I was to our relationship. Your first birthday after my release, for example: how badly I wanted to make that day special for you. I couldn't wait to take you shopping and treat you to a day on the town. I thought that day was going to be our big breakthrough, when in fact it was probably the beginning of the end. From that moment on, it felt as though everything between us was transactional—that the only value you saw in me was my ability to give you money and things. Some days that's how it felt. Stuff was our currency, not love. When your name popped up on my phone, I started to assume that you were calling me only for cash. Our relationship had been cheapened, reduced to thirty-dollar transactions, so I began to withdraw. I started sending you to voicemail. When I *did* answer the phone, it was with irritation and a dread of what you might be asking for this time. I stopped making a great effort to spend time with you in person.

And then disaster.

One day you called to say you needed more money, this time for a driver's license. When I refused, your voice rose and you told me that you would stab me.

Perhaps a man who had not been through what I'd been through would have processed your anger in a different way, but I was still trying to deal with something I didn't understand. I had been of the streets, and those streets had left me with untreated trauma, trauma as deep as any returning soldier's. When you threatened me with violence, I was triggered into the deeply buried ghosts of my life on the streets. I had been beaten; I had been shot; I had killed. I knew in my mind that I was no longer in prison or on the streets, but I didn't feel it, not yet—instead, I felt that familiar adrenaline, the chemicals that raged when someone disrespected me. It was a kind of madness, that anger. I could taste it, like blood in the mouth; it would take years to erase that taste, but back then, in my earliest days of freedom, I reacted as though I were still a captive.

And you were captive with me.

I called your grandfather and my best friends, Calvin and Fame, and told them what you had said. They tried to talk me down. You were just frustrated, they said, not processing your feelings in a healthy way. I listened, but I didn't feel them. So there was only one recourse: one of us had to go.

That was the trauma America had visited upon us, upon an entire generation of Black men. We coil tight like springs, inching toward oblivion with every slur we face, every confrontation. We didn't choose this way; it was etched on our faces like tattoos.

To even think, "One of us has to go," when for years I'd lain on my bunk dreaming of being a father to my son . . . that was what our culture had done to us. I found myself thinking back to when Reverend Marvin Gay, Sr., shot and killed his son, Marvin Gaye, the great singer. The elder Marvin had been an abusive father, and there was some kind of family argument that escalated into the son kicking and hitting his father. Marvin Sr. then fled the room, came back with a gun, and killed his son. There's a fine line between life and death, especially when guns are involved.

I understood all too well how anger and fear could spiral into violence. I, too, had pulled a trigger all those years earlier. I pictured your face, Jay, searching for the little boy that I had grown to love over the years, and, perhaps, searching in that face for my own innocent face. Could I find it? It was a practice I had learned in prison to defuse conflict, but the exercise was failing; the triggers were intoxicating. My ego had been sliced in a way that I hadn't experienced in nearly two decades. If I followed through with that thought—"One of us has to go"—I would end up back in prison, forever this time.

I decided to call your mother. Somewhere deep down I knew I wanted her to talk me off that terrible ledge. She knew the street side of me, and she understood you. Maybe she would have the words I needed to hear. She picked up, and before she could even say hi, I started yelling into the phone, "I'm going to put Jay in the trunk of a car and take him to Brightmo' and leave him over there fucked up! I'm tired of him disrespecting me and talking shit like I won't fuck him up! It's time for him to learn that I am not to be played with!"

Your mother pleaded with me not to hurt you, but I was filled with anger. My hands were the hands of a man who had lost it all once before. I knew the consequences of what I was threatening to do, but somehow I was comfortable with them; I knew how to survive prison.

Things weren't supposed to be like this between us. As a little boy you had been an artist, heading to school for graphic design. I dreamed of becoming a writer, with you designing all of my marketing materials. Our relationship was supposed to flow. When we fought, we would simply talk about our feelings and move on as father and son.

This would be our perfect story. It would be us against the world . . .

. . . but now it was us against each other. My son had been replaced by a broken young man, one I no longer recognized. And his father had been replaced by a man of prison, of the streets, saying "One of us has to go."

Still angry, I drove over to your neighborhood, looking for you. When I couldn't find you, I drove and drove and drove until I calmed down; then I turned my car toward home, where I eventually fell asleep. Waking in darkness, I couldn't imagine where it all would end.

A week later, I was pulling into my driveway when I got a call from your uncle Smiley.

Uncle Smiley was crying.

"Bro," he sobbed, "they killed Jay, they found his body over in Brightmo'. They kidnapped him from the gas station and took him over there and shot him."

The world ended there, as I sat in my car. My son was now dead. It was the universe paying me back, my nightmare come finally to life.

Then I thought of Sekou. What would I say to him, your little brother? How could I explain murder to him, much less the murder of his elder brother? There in that car, I could not move; my body was rigid with shock. I stared, my mind blank, until I noticed that there was enough gas in the car to drive to the coroner's office to identify your body. That was what my mind focused on: the fact that I had enough gas to drive to confirm your death.

But why was I even considering driving anywhere, with a river of tears pouring down my face?

Detroit has to be tired of consuming its young. That was the mantra I breathed as Jerry, a friend of mine, drove me to the gas station, the place where he said you had been kidnapped. The city flew by in a blur as we drove by block after block of burnt-out houses and buildings. *Detroit has to be tired of consuming its young.*

When we got to the station, I could see through the windows that a group of people had gathered inside, all of them waiting silently. I assumed they were your friends. I could see nothing in front of me; I was like a newborn with no vision. I approached someone—was it the owner of the station?—and told him I was your father. He just shook his head and said he was sorry about what had happened to you. I asked him if he had a tape from his security cameras, but he told me the police had already retrieved it and that I had to go down to the precinct.

As I looked around the room, my eyes started to clear. None of the people looked familiar, and I realized that there were so many elements of your life that I knew nothing about, including who your friends were, what they looked like. They talked about you, how you'd hustle at the gas station; that made sense, given what I knew of you. Smiley wrapped his arm around my shoulder, and I sank into him. Just then, as we began to leave, a young man who had been standing off to the side by himself started telling a story about your interaction with his mother. He said she fed you and that you took care of her yard.

That made no sense. You were making money working at your grandmother Marie's resale shop and didn't need to be doing any landscaping.

Now I was confused and even more scared. I didn't know what to do next, so I went to the precinct. The homicide detective told me I had to go to the coroner's office to identify the body, but that office was already closed. I would have to wait till the next morning. I called a friend who worked homicide, and she told me that they did have a young man who fit the description of my Jay.

At that point I decided to go to your grandfather's house.

The thought of confirming your death to him was crippling, almost too much to bear. When I arrived at his house, the street was packed with the cars of family members. I fumbled around in my pocket for the keys; just as I got to the door, your mother called me. "He's here. Jay is alive," she said.

My body collapsed against the door. I breathed for what felt like the first time in hours. My vision cleared, the monsters stepped back, life came back into focus. It had all been a horrible misunderstanding; the missing young man was not you, Jay. You were alive. My son was alive. No longer did one of us have to go.

I had faced the fact of your going, and that small taste was enough. I could never fathom such a thing; a father should never have to bury his son. Though I was still learning about this new world, I knew it was not a world in which fathers seek to bury their sons.

I needed then, urgently, to see you. I wanted to hug you, see your skin, your smile; that little boy I had first met in the visiting room so many years ago. But as much as I wanted those things, I also knew there were monsters we would have to confront. How could I move past the triggering effects of your threats, and how could you move past what I imagine must have felt like the appearance of an intrusive stranger in your life?

We had a lot of work to do. But you were alive, and for now, that was enough. I went inside and hugged your grandfather. We held each other, two generations hoping we could build a better future for a third—for you.

Yours,
Dad

Love Is Unconditional

When love beckons to you, follow him,
Though his ways are hard and steep.
—Kahlil Gibran, *The Prophet*

Dear Sekou,

Words seldom come close to the feelings behind them, but I want to start this letter by reminding you of one thing: I love you. Being your father is the greatest privilege the world has afforded me.

When your cells began to divide in your mother's womb, I was a couple of months shy of a year from being out of prison. Already I knew that you would be an extraordinary addition to our beautiful, broken planet. I could sense your magic, your divinity, the great gift of your being growing each day and, as it grew, helping grow in me a new place, a place that you would fill to the brim.

How did I know all that? To answer that, I would need to understand the secrets of the universe. (Spoiler alert: I do not understand the secrets of the universe.) The love you feel for a child is elemental, the DNA of the planet. A lot of people believe in a divine power; others believe in the power of nature; but to me, the greatest power that drives our world is the love we have for our children. There is no love so selfless, so complete, so overwhelming. Sure, not all parents feel that way about their child, but for most of us, the love of a child is the deepest, most fulfilling love we'll ever feel. It is different from love for a romantic partner, for a friend, or for a sister or brother or mother or father. It springs up unaided. It is chemical; we have no choice but to become as boring as hell as we talk about how great our kids are. I make no apologies for that. From the second you appeared in my life, the world had a different hue. I had to know you were safe at all times. There isn't a moment when I don't think about where you are, what you're doing, if you're okay, if you're happy, if you need something.

You are the purest part of me, the purest part of your mother, and the purest part of the two of us combined. You are wrapped in beautiful brown skin. You glint a dazzling smile so easily, and your golden spirit draws people close. Sekou, I love your musical laughter, your inherent intelligence, and your sense of humor. No matter where I am in the world, the simple thought of you causes my heart to grow.

Son, love is the most powerful emotion we have, because it inspires us to give our all and sacrifice everything for those we care about. Love is sacred because it comes from the most authentic space inside of us. But love is not honored by everyone—in fact, in some cultures, love is seen as weak, an emotion that proves weakness. For men especially, love can be seen as antithetical to our power, to our sense of masculinity, to the power we think we own. All this is bogus, garbage. It keeps men locked in a cold and lonely place. To my mind, loving someone is a sign of strength, not weakness. It takes huge amounts of courage to love, because to love is to trust and believe in the greater good and to do so in a world in which trust is shattered. If you had told the boy I was, facing imprisonment for a terrible crime, that one day he would sit on a couch with his beautiful son by his side, listening to him read from a book, watching his perfect brown fingers curl around the edges of the pages, his sweet voice burbling along the words—and that I would feel all the love in the world—well, I might have described such a scene as either impossible or a sign of a weakness I could never allow.

What I know now is that this is strength; this is power; this is fulfillment—sitting here, listening to you read.

There's a checklist of things fathers are supposed to give their sons: things like clothing, shelter, and food. But there is one key thing missing from the lists I've read: I need to give you high-level access to your emotions. Your power lies in your ability to grasp and unleash the power of being an emotionally evolved human being.

The martial arts sage Bruce Lee instructed his students, "Be formless, be shapeless, like water." Though he was talking about combat, I think this also applies to emotions. Water can take so many forms, from the deepest permafrost to the lightest mist of rain. When you are in tune with your emotions, you get to be anything you want to be—lighter than air or as tough as the earth's crust. Think about what water is—a mixture of hydrogen, the lightest element in the periodic table, and oxygen, which makes up almost half of the earth's crust in the form of oxides. This is what you're called to be— strong enough to sustain the weight of 7.5 billion people yet light enough to drift beyond the stratosphere; a mixture of solidity and fancy, a boy whose imagination will open his heart to all he meets.

Son, the world doesn't always look like a place filled with love, but trust me, love is present. Across the years I have met so many wonderful and caring people—people who've helped me, challenged me, raised me up, loved me, listened to me, given me opportunities. Some I would even say saved me. Above them all is you.

The men I met when I was incarcerated—Gangster Al, Slim Hurney, Timothy Greer, and others—those men saw something redeemable in me that I didn't see in myself. They fed me with literature, with their interest and care, and they helped grow me into a man. Each had either served decades in prison or is still in prison, some for more than forty years. I was one of the youngest in those maximum-security facilities, yet they saw leadership in me, a man whom guys would rally around because I was able to express myself effectively. The books they gave me changed my life—from *Think and Grow Rich* by Napoleon Hill to Malcolm X's autobiography, the novels of Donald Goines, and manifestos by Huey P. Newton. Because I read so fast, they tended to not believe me when I said I'd finished; they would challenge me on the details, just in case I hadn't actually read it. That would lead to lengthy debates about so many things.

What still moves me is the fact that those men had all come

in with life sentences, yet they still mentored the young. Even if the world felt they were on the scrap heap, they didn't. They were determined to better both themselves and the younger men coming after.

I am passing their love on to you.

I understand that to you, this is just your life, these are just your days, this is just your natural way: to be kind and funny and interesting and goofy and thoughtful and loving and strong. I don't expect you to understand that these attributes are so powerful because you do not use them for effect; your purity of spirit is seen by everyone.

I watch you have conversations with people—real conversations, not dumbed down. I see people do a double take: "Wait—am I really talking to an eight-year-old?" Recently, I went to get some pictures framed for the house, and you got into a conversation with the woman behind the counter. Your little engineer brain kicked in, and you were asking the woman all about how she did what she did. She stopped measuring the frame and looked at you, mesmerized. I'm not even sure she believed what had just happened. When I went back a few days later to get my pictures, the woman seemed disappointed that you weren't with me.

You leave trails of impressions on people, strong trails that affect their lives. Recently you explained the physics of one of your spinning toys to a friend of mine, startling him with your brain and your insight. You reminded him—so he said later—of both the beautiful innocence of childhood and the ability of a child's mind to gobble up so much new information.

I used to be terrible in the mornings—don't talk to me until one in the afternoon, that kind of thing. I had good reason: it's hard to wake up in the morning when the first thing you hear is bars rattling open and desperate men rushing to the bathroom and fighting over toilets and showers. Each morning I would wake and think, "I'm here. The nightmare is still happening. It's playing out in real life, not on a TV."

But you have your mother's ability to get going first thing, and you've changed even that fundamental thing about me: I can deal with the A.M. now. When I was in prison, I dreaded mornings. Morning meant one more day in Hell. Sleep at least gave me some peace, a few hours' worth of dreams, a break from the grind of incarceration—and I came to prefer it. But now your morning energy fills me with hope not just for the day at hand but for the years to come. It's the opposite of that dread in my prison cell. Your connectivity and engagement are impossible to resist. Our days are beautiful together, and the best part comes when each day reaches its end.

Every night we do our affirmations. These words ensure that you know who you are in the world before the world tries to tell you something different. We started when you were eighteen months old. You were just babbling at that point, but we couldn't start early enough, and this was our house, and this was our new life, and there was never going to be enough time. Twenty years I'd lost; there was no time to waste.

This is what you say (and what I say back):

I'm great (Yes, you are). I'm awesome (Totally). I'm amazing (You amaze me every day). I'm thoughtful (I see that in everything you do). I'm loving (I feel loved by you so much). I'm caring (It staggers me how much you care). I'm funny (Actually, you're hilarious). I'm smart (Everyone says it). I'm a big boy (Getting bigger every day). I'm a soldier (In the war for love). I'm a warrior (You will change the world). I am Sekou.

Sometimes if I have company over, and being the great spark you are, you naturally enough want to stay up with the adults. The affirmations are the perfect way to get you to want to go to bed. It's the best food in the world, and I don't have to force it on you. Already you understand the power of these words, of the time we share, of the rhythm of the cadences that serve to build a strength in you that no one can take away, that no culture can kill, no prejudice can touch.

This may seem like a simple thing, but these affirmations are crucial in this fractured, violent America into which you were born.

As Black men growing up in America, the narrative about us is so distorted. We are only ever seen in a one-dimensional way—as trouble or danger or a problem to solve—and that's why these affirmations are so crucial. It's as though we are, and always have been, America's problem to solve.

But we know that we are much more complex than that. We are not America's problem. We're not even each other's problem. We're just people, not three-fifths but one; we're humans, fumbling and stumbling along on this brief, accidental journey. I'm a father, a single father, and also a successful businessman, writer, activist, even if the culture doesn't recognize me in those ways. It doesn't see, or refuses to see, the love and caring and nurturing things we fathers do; we are just a problem, a symptom of decay or of danger, merely because of the color of our skin.

It's fine to fight against individual injustices, and we must do so—but the wider issue is the instinctual cultural assumptions that so many hold. They will look at an innocent, beautiful boy—you, Sekou—and before they hear that you have empathy or wit or intelligence or gentleness or anything positive, they will assume that you are a problem to corral, a problem to solve, a problem to run from, a problem to lock up or even kill. This is our predicament, the disunion intrinsic to our union. Entire systems have been created to control this perceived problem, be it unfair housing, unfair hiring, unfair incarceration, unfair access to food and healthcare—and these systems free white culture to ignore the truth that you are a sweet boy to be cherished.

Everyone should know this: the system is weak compared to the power of a father's love and a child's self-belief. Though there are forces ranged against you, Sekou, and against all young Black boys, you and those boys have a much stronger force within yourselves. The affirmations we share every night are a crucial antidote to those pressures. One thing I understood was that if your mother and I could prepare you to understand who you are very early on, we could begin to make you bulletproof; our love for you could not only be a salve but also a shield.

Son, not only are you the future, you are the present, because your place on Earth right now—right here this very moment—is more important than anything else to me. You are a reflection of the many sons throughout the world who are making it a better place. You are a latecomer in a tradition that has fought oppression, broken chains, marched and sung and written and taken the brickbats of a culture that sees us as only partly human and sometimes not even partly. But despite all this heavy history at your back, you are innocent. I will do everything to let that innocence continue for as long as I can. Thank you for bringing me so much laughter and light. Thank you for inspiring me to work harder to ensure that your future is secured. Above all, thank you for allowing me to fully be the father and man I am destined to be.

Love always,
Daddy

Racism

Dear Jay and Sekou,

This letter is about the shit that we carry with us that people don't understand; what's simply called racism. I hate to have to describe it to you, but you'll know soon enough in any case.

The *word* the world uses is racism—or discrimination or injustice—but I'd say it's deeper than the indignity of being measured by the color of one's skin. Sure, racism seems to be at the root of this country's engagement with the Black community: the way opportunities are barred to us, the overpolicing, the violence we face, the casual way our culture expects us to be a problem. But there is something even more invasive and dangerous that we experience: the overwhelming feeling of *dread*. When we encounter racism on a near-daily basis, it leaves us with a consistent, haunting feeling that we are about to be falsely accused, brutalized, or denied opportunities others see as their birthright. Are we going to be stereotyped just on the basis of the color of our skin? That stereotyping stems from the dread of us in the racist culture in which we find ourselves. As we fight to change that racist culture—a culture that enslaved, discriminated against, and lynched our ancestors—we must also work on that feeling of dread; we need to corral it, tame it, not let it dominate our lives. This constant vigilance is what tires our souls, and it's what I want to talk about.

That we live in a racist society is a statement no less true for being obvious. We are aware of the criminalization of Black males as a matter of public policy; we can all see how the media depict Black men as a threat, as uncontrollable, as fundamentally opposed to the good things in society. We hear the dog whistles about ungovernable cities, the threat to the suburbs, the vitriol about "making America great (i.e., white) again." Black boys and men are a force to fear. There is no nuance to us. We're fast or tall or strong or dangerous or sexual or angry or all of the above. We are not subtle, that's for sure. When one of us is shot dead by the police, every story makes sure to mention some distant criminal charge—what I call "the mugshot that has nothing to do with the moment." We are demonized. We don't protest, we loot. Even the idiosyncrasies of our language work to depict Blackness as problematic: people are blacklisted, black cats are bad luck, there are black ice on roads and black sheep in families, reputations are blackened, and it's all one big black mark upon our very name.

Beneath all the reduction and slur is the sense that Black communities are monolithic—that we are either rappers or sports stars or we're dysfunctional, angry, violent, a threat.

There's even less nuance when you're a felon. First up, housing: forget trying to rent (in most cases). Though there are laws against discriminating in the real estate market, there's no rule against not renting to a person with a felony. Sekou, when I first got out, your mom and I were finally able to rent an apartment from a woman who looked the other way when she ran my record, but in that neighborhood, my Ford Taurus was stolen twice in two weeks. (It had nice rims, what can I say?) We couldn't live in a place like that, not with a baby and your mom coming home late at night from work. But when we tried to move to somewhere safer, once again the applications were denied. Eventually I found a way to get a home outside of the usual mortgage route, but even then, I could barely get house insurance—and when we moved to this new house in Los Angeles, even though I applied through USAA via my dad's military service, still I was turned down.

But the problems didn't end with insurance and apartments. Getting a job wasn't easy, either. After one interview, I was told straight out that because of my felony, the company didn't feel comfortable hiring me.

I was exhausted from running from the reality of my past. These are the macroproblems, but the microtraumas are what really drive the exhaustion.

When we got Indyego, Sekou, you were so excited. I hope you always remember how much it meant to set eyes on that puppy that first day. I wasn't sure about getting a dog, but he's pretty cute with those light inverted commas framing his marblelike gray eyes. He's added so much love and light to our lives already. There's a purity to an animal that we human animals have lost. A dog can remind you of the instinctual element of love that too often gets harassed into pain.

But even having a dog isn't unalloyed joy; not when we're forever having to prove something about ourselves as a race.

Let me explain what I mean. Recently when you were staying with your mom, Indy got sick and shit all over his cage in the middle of the night. Usual puppy stuff. He looked so sad, so I got him out, cleaned him off, then took the cage out into the Los Angeles night to sort it out in the driveway. I'm not the biggest fan of cleaning dog shit out of a cage at 3:00 A.M., but it had to be done.

After rinsing the thing out, I realized that I was making a lot of noise, what with the cage and the water hose and me cursing my luck. All of a sudden, in a great rush of realization, I understood the danger I was in: Here I was, a Black man in a dark driveway, making noise in a nice West LA neighborhood in the middle of the night. All it would take would be one concerned citizen to call it in, and suddenly there would be a bunch of squad cars in my driveway. I'd be told to keep my hands where they could be seen, and I'd be asked for my ID. "Well, Officer, I don't tend to carry ID when I'm cleaning shit out of a dog crate at three in the morning. . . . And can I prove I live here? Well, I can, but only if you let me into my house to show you my ID." And round and round it goes, unless the officer gets jumpy, and then all bets are off.

This is what we live with all the time: something simple and already fairly degrading—cleaning up puppy shit—turns into something potentially dangerous. Or we're sitting in our car somewhere, taking in the sunrise or the sunset, and suddenly we don't have enough air in our tires or our blinker is out, and they can check your car, check your person, and run your life through that little computer that holds the keys to prisons all over America.

But despite all of this, despite the fear that sets in when I'm simply trying to exist, I want to believe in the best of what it means to be human. And I truly do believe we have the skill set to fix a lot of this; it doesn't have to be like this forever. That night at 3:00 A.M., as the last bit of Indyego's shit swirled down the drain, I calmed myself, preparing to stay cool for the world, to soak in the nighttime—anything I could not to internalize these fears so deeply that I couldn't process them. If you internalize them, you'll never have happiness and fulfillment because you'll never feel truly safe, truly free.

But it doesn't mean that the thoughts don't come, and that's where our frustration builds. Too often we find ourselves trying to explain this to our friends, this sense of dread; we have to consciously work on these thoughts, pushing them into their corner. Just imagine this: a Black man in a nice car, being followed by a police car. Do I have my insurance? Do I have my license? Is everything up to date? Should I take my baseball cap off? Or how about in a high-end store? Being followed all the way around the place until finally the clerk asks, "Can I help you?" These are the exhausting things.

One morning after the Ahmaud Arbery and George Floyd murders, I stepped outside our home to get the mail, and I froze. I had a hoodie on. What if one of my neighbors called the police? All this from a hoodie. What is my story if the police show up? Will I be approached as a homeowner or a suspect? The only way I've found to combat this is to remain mindful, to tell myself, "This isn't happening, this isn't your reality. Not all people are racist; not all cops are assholes."

I learned that a couple of years ago in Cincinnati.

It was a Friday night. I was standing outside a barbershop with a small group of mostly Black men.

That year, the Smithsonian had organized a traveling exhibit called Men of Change, which I had been lucky enough to be featured in. Wherever the exhibit went, barbershops in the community could enter a contest to win $10,000 to rehab the place. Community barbershops are one of the key places where change can be made; they're often the lifeblood and center of Black communities. So as part of our tour, we were bouncing around to the barbershops, starting with the launch in Cincinnati. That particular night we were joined by Jerome Bettis, who played for the Pittsburgh Steelers, and Roland Martin, a radio and TV personality.

At one point I went out to smoke a cigar with a couple of guys, and within two minutes I noticed a young white police officer approaching us. He was talking out loud to himself. From what I could make out, he was saying "What the fuck? Nobody is fucking impeding traffic here." He had a look of total disgust on his face, as though he couldn't believe he'd had to follow up some bullshit call. Apparently some car had passed us, and the driver had seen three Black men standing on the corner in front of the barbershop and called the police, saying we were blocking traffic with a car. (There was no car.)

As the officer reached us, I just said, "Hey, how's it going today?"

At that, he stopped and looked me in the face. "Man, it's

just this dumbass call, and I have to follow up," he explained. I could tell from the start that he was as annoyed as we were.

I nodded. "Man, I get it. But nobody's impeding traffic here. I was just out here smoking a cigar and celebrating this barbershop thing. In fact, you should come inside."

He seemed tempted—amazed, even—but he said he didn't want to ruin the fun by stepping in. "If I walk in, your party goes flat," he said. We both nodded in acknowledgment of the reality of the distrust between the community and police officers.

I liked the man. He had a soul, and he was sensitive to the bullshit he'd been fed by the caller. When I asked him how long he'd been on the force, he said ten months. "You should really come in, then," I told him. "If you're going to be patrolling around here, barbershops are a staple in the community."

When he still demurred, I mentioned to him that Jerome Bettis and Roland Martin were inside, and at that he pretty much lost his mind. "You gotta be shitting me! The Bus is in there?"

At that, I sent someone in to get Jerome and explained to him when he came out that this officer had looked past the bullshit to see the human beings in front of him. Jerome shook his hand, and the cop said, "Man, if my dad was still alive, he would be so excited. You were his favorite player." It was a wonderful moment of hero worship, of fathers and sons and humanity, and I sensed then a kind of breaking, a fissure in the pain we all carried around with us.

Unbeknown to me, a friend, Ernest Sisson, took a picture of the moment. In it, you can see the wide-eyed innocence of a young white cop realizing, I think, that life was going to be more complex, interesting, and beautiful than he could ever have imagined. (Oh, and by the way, he's no longer a cop.)

When I wrote about that incident a few months later, it instantly went viral—and that's because, I think, it was one of those moments that reminded all of us of our humanity, our frailties, and our similarities. In that moment we were all just men navigating the world without the mask we'd been trained to wear. I could have taken offense, called out the officer, and accused him of being a racist cop; he could have believed the caller and acted based on stereotypes about Black men in groups. Instead, somehow, we chose to just see each other and talk like humans. It's ultimately a decision we can all make. When he lit up like a kid at seeing his dad's sports hero, I saw a little boy, and his uniform no longer mattered. We shared, then, a commonality that could transcend his place in life and mine, taking us back to a childhood when we were all innocent and hopeful and our dads were our unadulterated heroes.

We chose to see beyond the uniforms we were wearing. We can always choose this.

Not everyone is out to get you, but the reality remains: you are Black men. You fit the description. I can't tell you how many times I get into a limo and the driver asks if I'm a rapper or do I play football? Hotel check-ins? Same. (Sometimes it's easier to get my white colleagues to check if my room is ready.) Because of the nature of my work, I'm often the only Black man in a lot of white spaces. At hotels and resorts and conferences, oftentimes the only other Blacks I see are in the service industry. My white peers' experience of these settings is very different from mine.

It's not just that I'm ignored; I'm actually made to feel invisible. As I'm waiting for a table in a restaurant, a group of white people will come in after me and the maître d' will walk right past me to tend to them first. When I first moved into an apartment building in Hollywood, my midwestern soul found it natural to say hello to folks in the elevator, but it was a rare thing to be acknowledged, let alone get a hello back. When I got a puppy, things changed a bit—people were quite happy to say hello (to the puppy). Compare that to when a Black person does something notable; then he can't help but be seen.

Even allies can miss the mark. Sometimes I'll get calls after one of those awful high-profile assaults or murders—"If only he hadn't resisted" or "But his record suggests he was violent." Do I assume that these people are racist? If so, what good will it do me?

Even when you're in a legitimate space for a legitimate reason, the white culture can still swoop in and question you. I was out back at the Grammys when a white woman came up to me and asked, "Hey, which group are you? Are you a solo artist?" When I said no, she asked, "So do you work for an artist?"

"Nope. Just here with friends," I said.

"Did you sneak in?" she asked with a side-eye.

She was fixated on how I had gotten into the Grammys. There had to be a reason, given that I'm Black—it couldn't just be that, like her, I was just there. A writer? Sorry, don't get it. I can't be a writer, a consultant, a thinker, a teacher, a professor.

In that moment, I could have called her out as racist or I could have called out the entire culture that gives her the right to question me—and what's the betting she's got "tons of Black friends"? The bottom line is, what you realize in such moments is that we're constantly being delegitimized.

Then there was the time I was flying back from Boston to Los Angeles. Right off the plane, two white guys—so obviously plainclothes cops that it was almost comical—were watching everyone walk along the concourse. One of them approached me and asked, "Are you Terry?" What the fuck? "No, I'm not Terry," I said, at which point he asked to see my ID.

I just kept on walking. He had no right to see my ID, and he and I both knew it. But he wouldn't let it go—that's the nature of the culture, it won't let us go. He followed me along the hallway, trying to get my ID. (I'm sure Terry made a clean getaway; you're welcome, Terry.)

In the end I said, "You don't know who the fuck you're looking for, so you just harassed the first Black guy to get off the fucking plane?" His sense of entitlement was so strong, he didn't even feel the need to make something up. "Yes, that's basically it," he said. "You gotta be the stupidest mother-fucker ever," I said, and kept on going. The encounter didn't escalate, fortunately (because I would have been in the wrong, no question—that's how it is), but to anyone watching from a distance—the people I'd just flown with for five hours, all now passing me on their way home, casting glances at me—I was clearly the bad guy, when in reality the idiot simply didn't know how to do his job.

The dread is constant. Even though I knew I was in the right, still I found myself thinking, "Is everything straight? Did I do something in Boston? Do I have weed?"

The continuous pricks at our identity are agonizing. How am I to navigate them? How are you to do so? If you don't have the mechanism to self-affirm or reimagine who such people are—for example, that they are victims of cultural ignorance inside a racist system rather than merely racist—you will find life unbearable, and we must avoid the ledge. It's exhausting to have to make your own journey peaceful at all times—to walk into a room with confidence when the entire culture is against you. That's why affirmations are so important, and that's why friends and allies are so important, too, because they value you as a human being first and only.

I want to believe in the best of what it means to be human. So I just try to prepare every second I can and stay cool for the world, soaking things in and letting the pain drip off me whenever I can. We have to learn to process the pain, because if all you do is internalize it, you'll never have happiness and fulfillment because you'll never feel safe.

People are yearning for the good. Most people want to see racial reconciliation. How can we get there? For me, the journey began with one step: resolving the puzzle in my head. Thinking back to that night in Cincinnati, my typical response to a cop might well have been "Well, what the fuck you want from us now?" On the cop's side, he was probably thinking "Fuck, now I'm already here, and my presence is a threat to them." But as each of us worked out the other's humanity, I remember seeing the wave of relief cross his face; we were present to each other as two human beings.

I didn't escalate the incident, but that wasn't even my job. It had already been escalated. We had been called in as a threat, and then the cop had had to come by, escalating further. There had already been three distinct escalations in that situation, none of them due to me. The culture escalates without effort.

What matters is not escalation or de-escalation—it's mindfulness, which I see as the gateway to reconciliation. Mindfulness is a practice in which you bring yourself completely to the present moment; you check the narrative that's constantly running in your head and recognize what's happening right in front of you as well as inside of you. Instead of telling the woman at the Grammys to go fuck herself, I brought myself to the realization that it was my first time at the Grammys, and on that particular night they would be paying homage to Kobe Bryant, who'd died that same morning. That was what mattered, not some random person questioning how I had gotten in.

In moments like this, mindfulness—not the woo-woo, softy-softy kind but a real and intense effort to play witness to actions and feelings with clarity and calmness—is the first step not only to solving the painful event but to gaining an internal peace. It's crucial to realize that what happens inside us is more important than what's happening in the material world around us. Reconciliation begins with fixing what's inside. It creates space for an authentic beauty in which we can be honest with friends—and random cops—about the nuance of our existence. When we talk about such incidents, you'll find that real friends can hold a space for the facts. They will love you for you, not for your ability to fight against this or that or the other.

I can see you rolling your eyes. At what point are we allowed to be human and it doesn't cost our fucking life? Well, here we are, the children of four hundred years of agony. We can only allow ourselves to be human and care for our own internal narratives while hoping that others will eventually follow. Be mindful for the sake of your sanity so that you can be fully present in the world, even when it feels as though the world doesn't welcome your presence.

If we're going to heal, we have to stand in the truth; we can't hide from these tough conversations. What does it take to heal? Radical honesty. Because we always have a choice. We can choose to ignore or get angry or let the bile of racism fill our throats. Or we can choose to be entirely present with those around us, entirely open to honest conversations, loving but firm, known as someone who stands for something at all times. It's a lot harder than just showing up now and then, but it's what the current situation calls for. Our engagement with one another and with these big questions shouldn't be something we save for Sundays or marches or every four years when an election comes around. Our highest ideals should be the clothes we wear every single day, a uniform we never take off.

Oh, and don't forget—in moments that could go either way, it helps to have Jerome Bettis behind you in a barbershop.

Dad

The Hoop in the Driveway

Dear Sekou,

Yesterday, I was sitting in my garage listening to music when I heard your mother's car roll up our driveway. I'd been without you for a few days. Though I'd gotten plenty of work done, seen friends, and had the damn TV all to myself, I knew something elemental was missing from my life. With our shared co-parenting, your mother and I face this goodbye-hello-hello-goodbye all the time, but it's only when you're gone that I realize what a force of love you are and how much I miss it, and you.

The driveway at the side of our house is sepa-rated from the garage by a huge wooden gate. From the other side, I heard your trilling voice shouting, "Daddy!" As I ran toward you, I called you "Poopy-Doopy," because that's what dads do. I hit the latch, the gate swung open, and there you were with your backpack and your cool sneakers and the smile that lights up half of Los Angeles. Your mother and I chatted about things parents chat about: her not having had time to wash your hair, my needing to remind you to submit your homework. A lovely excitement charged the air among the three of us, as in just one week we would be celebrating your ninth birthday. You kissed your mother goodbye and bounced into the yard, already looking forward, I think, to being back in our house.

You love your time with your mom, of course, but I like to think you're happy to come back here, too, to your couch and your bed and your big-ass TV and your chess set and your everything.

As you bounded into the house, I waited out in the garage awhile to ponder on my love for you. Sometimes I have to take a moment to breathe, to rearrange the molecules in me that are jangled by your presence. The way your arm lifts just so to open the door; the way your fingers grasp the handle; the little push of power in your legs as you lean and shift it open, tumbling into the house with all the fervor and innocence of an eight-year-old about to be nine. Your voice from the living room: "Daddy," you call, "Daddy, can I have thirty minutes of time?" This is our code for your time to decompress, to hang out in the house playing a game or watching a TV show, a chance to waste half an hour with no agenda in the crucial endeavor of "being home." The thirty minutes resuscitate you and let the air settle around you—comfort and safety and presence falling on you like the lightest of invisible blankets: love.

So I wait and listen and let you have your thirty minutes. I, too, need that time to prepare to be totally present, to put aside work and advocacy and, yes, my past—I work during those thirty minutes to recenter myself as a father, not as

Shaka Senghor. Being a father means building a scaffold of love upon which your child can climb; in the days you've been away, I have dismantled some of that scaffold so that I don't go crazy from missing you.

There is a trope in our culture of the absent father and the sainted single mother, but the reality for so many of us is actually agony. Do you really think we want to be away from our children? Who would choose such a thing? Relationships end, and the culture is adamant that the mother shall take the lead in parenting and spending time with and nurturing. There are very few courts or judges who, all things equal, land upon the father as the most appropriate parent, and so we have learned to take the second road, to acquiesce to the image of us as less than, as inadequate to the task of love. We are not inadequate to it. We yearn for it, but so often we find ourselves out here in the garage of our lives, away from the main rooms, steeling ourselves for either loss or reentry.

I tell you this, Sekou, with no bitterness. I just wish fathers could change that narrative a bit and be seen as equal to the love of mothers. But such thoughts are dispelled as you come running out of the house, leap across my chest into my arms, and say, "Daddy, we need to make a list!" Such enthusiasms—instant, passionate, real—are what children bring to our dark world. There are groceries to get, and when you ask me if it's okay if you make the list, though I fear what it will contain—pizza, probably, and what else?—of course you can make it. This is your effort to regain your home, to fill it with nourishment, and because you are a darling boy, you make sure to remember the things I want to eat and drink. I tell you about a ginger ale from Detroit called Vernors, and

how sometimes Ralph's has it. (In Detroit, Vernors isn't just a
soda; it is believed to fix all and any ailments. Got a headache?
Drink Vernors. Upset stomach? Drink Vernors. Hell, it might
even kill Covid.) The fact that Ralph's may have a bottle of
this drink/potion is enough to excite you beyond all reason,
because what if Ralph's *does* have Vernors and you can try it,
and also can we get pizza? Of course we can, because pizza
is the shortest way I know to making it clear that I love you.

But before we shop, we decide to head out to shoot some
hoops. I got pretty good in prison until I tore my ACL. (In
prison, there's no way you're getting surgery for a torn ACL;
the best you can hope for is some Motrin.) In the yard, I
would drain and drain and drain without really trying, but
you at just eight are showing signs of talent, too. You bring
your right hand up high, and, *whoosh*, you hurl that ball, and
it clangs off the backboard and in. You remind me of a game
we played a few weeks earlier and how here [points to a spot
on the yard] was three point and here [different spot] was
two and here [up close] was just one and how we scored hundreds of points, and your memory takes me back to a different
yard, the bumping and hustling and aggression that filled our
games—a loveless, desperate sport inside a loveless, desperate
place—and how far I've come. Here we are, enjoying a simple
game of basketball in a yard in our house in Los Angeles, but
quickly I find myself thinking about love and how the boys
and men with whom I lived in prison displayed such little of
it toward themselves. How could they, given the degradation
of their pasts, the degradation of their daily lives inside?
As I learned their stories, I came to appreciate how a lack

of self-love had often led to the bad decisions and pain that brought them to this place.

I think about those guys every time we play. For you, it's just a fun activity with your dad, but for me, and for many of those men, it's a crucial salve against the brutality of our lives.

I've always been a huge basketball fan. I grew up a Pistons nut, from the bad-boy era. I especially loved Isiah Thomas—not the biggest but the boldest. As he once said, he was never chasing Michael Jordan, it was the other way round. (Thomas already had two championships before Jordan got his first.) But as much as I love the sport and was good at it and would love to pass that on to you, we're not boxed into that endeavor—in fact, I hope in some ways that you don't need basketball to give you a sense of hope and wonder about the world. If we didn't spend the time shooting hoops, we'd spend it together doing something else. The point is connection, is joy, and we don't need basketball to help with that. So far, you don't really give a shit about basketball beyond this driveway, and that's fine by me. It's the time together that matters.

So on we go, shooting hoops, here in this LA yard, just a couple of miles from the home of the Lakers, who had just won the championship; LeBron's fourth, three with different teams. He, too, had succeeded against the odds. He was from Akron, less than 200 miles from Detroit, born to Gloria, his mother, when she was sixteen. His father was absent, the family struggled to make ends meet, and Gloria knew it would be better for LeBron to live with a local youth football coach than with her. Imagine her having to make that decision; giving up her son to secure him a future. Now there he is just a few miles from us, winning it all for the fourth time.

These are the things I think about as you throw the ball up into the air toward the hoop in this game by which men have made something out of nothing.

Toward the end of my sentence, my friend Calvin and I created a class based on the ideas in the book *Houses of Healing: A Prisoner's Guide to Inner Power and Freedom* by Robin Casarjian. Initially we invited just six guys to meet and talk about their feelings, and it was incredible to witness their outpouring about parental abuse, violence, neglect, and PTSD. Those men cried for the first time in their adult lives, and eventually the group grew from six to a full capacity of twenty-five, all sharing stories and hugging each other. I could see then that there was a need for men to heal—and to be loved, truly loved by other men in a real and honest and accepting way.

Back then, I dreamed of having someone care as much about me as I care about you now and as much as you care about me. There's a song by Nas called "One Love," in which he talks about caring for his friend who is on lockdown. I remember lying on my bunk listening to that song and bolting straight up with a shock of recognition, realizing that that was the kind of love I was missing: someone to leave fifty bucks in the commissary for me, or just someone to tell me to "rise up above." I wanted someone to write me a letter, to tell me the news from home and say that they were thinking about me. I wanted someone to come visit me. I wanted someone to believe in me even though I had hit the rockiest of bottoms.

The truth back then was that most of my friends had abandoned me. There were no letters, no visits, nothing to remind me that I had been a full human before incarceration. And that hurt so much; it took me years to realize that the truth was that they didn't really love themselves. The reality is that they had suffered the same kind of childhood trauma, abuse, and gun violence that I had. That made it nearly impossible for them to be there for me because they still hadn't worked out how to be there for themselves. Not their bad; not mine. When you are betrayed or hurt early in life by those who are supposed to care for you, it makes it hard to believe that you are worthy of love.

Sekou, from the moment you were born, I knew I wanted to break that cycle and introduce love into your life in a healthy way.

Which is why, though it may be true that we need to go grocery shopping and clean up the house a little, and it may be true that I have calls to make and work to do and you probably have homework, too, we'll stay out here a little longer, shooting hoops, because I can think of nothing better, nothing more innocent, nothing more meaningful than you rearing back, hurling that ball up into the air from the three-point spot, and watching it arc into the basket like a meteor of joy.

I love you.

Dad

Freedom Is My Legacy

Dear Jay,

It's been ten years since I walked out of prison a partially free man. I say partially free because there is no such thing as full freedom for a man who has served time. There are the obvious repercussions: the two years of parole, the threat of being reincarcerated for nothing at all, the constraint of not being able to travel out of state without permission. These rules create an awful kind of muscle memory. I remember hearing the story of Bakithi Kumalo, the South African bass player. When Paul Simon brought him over to New York from apartheid South Africa to play on the *Graceland* album, Kumalo asked where the nearest police station was so he could register. That was what Blacks had to do in his homeland, and it's what I have to do in mine. We're horrified when we hear about the degradations of apartheid, but there are other, less obvious blocks to freedom: the inner terrors, the everyday experience of being denied basic rights, things that take a lifetime to seep away—if they ever do.

But those first months . . . even though I had to go to the parole office before I did anything, when I talked to Ebony the night before and she told me you were going to be joining her to pick me up, I got so excited. In my mind, it was working out to be the perfect homecoming. Do you remember that day? It is a blur to me, just as some of the first few days kind of merge together like cars on the freeway during rush-hour traffic.

So much had changed since I'd been incarcerated in 1991. The Internet had become a thing only after I had gone to prison. Amazon.com had launched in 1995, and DVDs had shown up around the same time. The iPod, now pretty much obsolete itself, hadn't shown up until 2001. Any portable phones I'd known had been cinder blocks; now everyone carried a pocket-sized computer that could facilitate talking to anyone on the planet at any time. Imagine, then, the shock of adjusting to life in June 2010, when I was finally released. I once described myself as being like Fred Flintstone stepping into an episode of *The Jetsons*.

I went into prison as a kid, and I came out with the naiveté of a kid. Being away for so long creates a kind of arrested development; it's seen regularly in women and men who go away when they are young and come back decades later. It wasn't as if I hadn't been through trauma and harsh realities of my own, realities that had matured me in my own way. I had taken care of myself while in prison, but there were still some experiences I just hadn't had, couldn't have had given that I'd been incarcerated. I'd never had a bank account; never had a legitimate job; never had a driver's license; never had a car in my own name.

Most of what I thought I knew about life was based on ideas I had formulated from reading books and magazines. There were none of the trials and errors that come with living life. Things like ordering in a fancy restaurant; knowing the dress code for an interview (I hadn't worn a suit since being sentenced in 1991); navigating a Word document (I thought Microsoft Word *was* the Internet); or going on a date (a date that required flowers and planning). I could only imagine how I would respond, react, and act in this life on the outside. And though I knew the facts of your life outside, I hadn't lived through those things with you. Your life was a tale told to me secondhand, not something we'd shared.

When I first stepped out of the parole office into the parking lot, I remember feeling as though we—you, me, Ebony, all of us—were about to conquer the world. I also remember wanting to set the tone for what I imagined our future together would look like. I wanted you to know that I was truly a man of my word. So many of the men who had gotten out before me had talked about what they were going to do when they got home—some wanted to be real estate investors, some musicians, some business owners, everything you could imagine. But year after year, I had watched many of those men with hopes come back into prison, their plans and dreams and hopes crushed like old cars in a junkyard. Being jailed is antithetical to the human spirit; it works to kill the spirit. I think we can all stop lying that prison is about rehabilitation—for centuries, and especially in this one, its chief function has been to punish and mar the human spirit in an act of monstrous revenge.

It was disheartening. What did it mean for those of us still in prison who harbored our own hopes and dreams? Would we face the junkyard, too? It was terrifying to consider. "Outside" held such an allure for us, but we saw that "outside" was harsh and unwelcoming and could crush a man. Brilliant, talented men were regularly coming back to a life of hell.

What were we to do with that information? Should we bury it as we did so much of the trauma we faced? Should we reassess our dreams? Should we stop dreaming altogether? Should we just assume that the outside world would render us useless, broken, crushed into boxes of metal? In the face of the men returning, their eyes a little more dead than before, I remember telling myself that their fate wasn't going to be my fate. But inside me, deep deep inside me, there was a voice telling me that I wasn't any different from them. "Who are you," the voice asked, "to think that you can escape the fate of these great men returning? What is it about you, Shaka, that will make you strong enough to not return? Do you have that soul? Have you created that soul in your writings, in your dreams, in your hopes for the future? Are you that man, Shaka?"

That voice didn't ruin me, though. In fact, I worked even harder to make sure I proved it wrong. I wanted you to see that the things I'd said to you in letters and visits and calls were real. I would live by them and enact them with you and for you.

I hated that voice inside me, but I knew, too, that it would save me. It would keep my eyes alive.

★ ★ ★

Now I was outside, and though the voice could sometimes chill me, I also knew that I would have to get past the parties and celebrations and set the tone for what I wanted the future to look like. I had dreamed of running my own business for years and couldn't wait to get started.

I will never forget my first book sale with you there in the parking lot at the parole office. Do you remember? I had met the brother I sold the book to during the last sixty days inside prison, in the dayroom at Mound Correctional Facility. We had talked about the countdown to freedom as though we were old friends, just two men facing down the dead eyes of the men who had returned. I remember telling that man I wanted to be an author when I got out, and he said he wanted to support me and would push my books for me. In my mind, I imagined that we would connect after we were home for a while, but he said he wanted to buy a book the very day we were released.

Can you imagine what that felt like, what that did to my soul? I'm filled with pride when I think about that first sale out of the trunk of a car. I had shown that I wasn't going to be crushed like a useless vehicle, I was going to sell a book and sell it to a brother who had come home like me. Beyond how important that was to my soul, there was also the symbolism of the sale as a sign to you of what I was going to be, what I was going to represent. I wanted to impress upon you that I was serious about building a life of accomplishment and that I was coming home to put in real work.

Did you see that? Did that prove to you that I was going to make it outside and not be crushed like so much old metal?

★   ★   ★

From that moment to this day, I haven't stopped pushing for my dream. But I have grown into a deeper realization of what I needed to be for you. You didn't need to see me stick to a plan for myself, didn't need me to set an example of work ethic or be an entrepreneur or writer or a man outlasting his prison to be something notable and someone to look up to. The truth is, I was so caught up in my own shit that I hadn't considered that maybe all you really needed was for me to just be present.

Jay, this is the complexity of being a parent. Sometimes we can be seduced into thinking that our dreams of making it, whatever that means—our successes, our accolades and triumphs—are the best gifts we can give our children. The truth is, that's just what my friend Dr. Shefali calls "parenting with our ego attached." Our entire culture tells us that that's what parents are for—to be heroes, running into fires, making money, getting the corner office or the record deal, winning at life. But the truth is, parents just need to be there for their children. They need to stop what they're doing when their child talks, and they need to listen. Looking back, there are so many things that I wish I could have done differently as your father. I wish I had spent more time explaining to you why I was going so hard to make my dreams happen—I was running, yes, running from my past, but I was also running from the fear of returning to the streets and going back to prison. I was running from the image of those men I'd seen return, their dead eyes, their dreams of "outside" crushed. And it wasn't just that I was running from reincarceration. No, I was running because I was afraid of what a return would do to me, knowing that the system had won. It had been ahead of me for so long; it had run up the score; there were just a few minutes left and the buzzer was approaching, and could I really force a comeback? Could I really run the ball up the court and make the shot that said I was a man, free, unbeaten, and unbeatable? I knew I had to keep moving, pushing, forging ahead.

In prison there was only one thing I was afraid of, and that was losing my mind. That fear remained even after I was on the outside. I thought back to so many moments when I realized I'd been incarcerated to be broken. One day I was talking to an officer who had come to my cell to do a routine shakedown. He discovered that I had more books and toiletries than allowed and demanded that I send them home. He wouldn't even allow me to pass the books to others on the block or share the toiletries. It was such a dumb policy, barring us from helping our fellow prisoners with things they couldn't afford.

I was incensed—how could this person be in control of me, of all of us? I was smarter, more inquisitive, more analytical than this guy would ever be, but somehow he was able to lock me into a cage, dictate what I would eat, when I would go to bed—in fact, he had complete control over my life and my fate. If he wanted to be violent toward me, the system would let him. He could come in and shake down the cell whenever he wanted to, throw my belongings on the floor, put things I'd legitimately bought into the trash, deny me food in solitary, and put sworn enemies into the same cell. He could throw away my mail or deny visits for no reason. If he wanted to dehumanize me with a word, he could do so with no sanction.

In that moment, I promised myself that I would never again put myself into a situation where my life would be controlled by someone who was barely intelligent enough to tie his own shoes. The thought of going back to a space where that was the daily reality was frightening as hell.

So this was what I did: once I was outside, I hit every park, every barbershop, and every strip club I could think of and tried to sell books to anyone and everyone I encountered— including the Jehovah's Witnesses who came to my door (true story).

I was taking all of the shit I had learned in the streets and on prison yards and adding it to what I knew people might call "legitimate." I had studied marketing and read books like *Think and Grow Rich*. On the back of what I'd learned, I set up readings and book signings and sold fifteen to twenty books each time—sometimes more, sometimes less. I offered people, including you, the opportunity to hustle and make five dollars per book sold. Some were unwilling to hustle, so I got out there myself. I tried everything from multilevel marketing to selling T-shirts. My new friend Clement "Fame" Brown had a boutique on the west side, on Joy Road, and I opened a bookstore in the front of the store, next to the clothes Fame had designed.

But the truth was this: I needed merely to be present for you. Yes, I wanted you to see me making my way in the world after two decades inside, but I should also have just sat with you, let you talk, let you be, let our lives just mesh quietly, away from commerce and books and dreams of success. Remember the time I took you with me to my old neighborhood in Brightmo'? I was selling books at Motor City Java House; I was so happy to have you with me, this tall and beautiful boy. I was excited to see the Jay that I'd heard so much about—the jokester, the charming hustler, the artist

and hard worker. I thought it was the beginning of our tour-
ing the world, and I couldn't have been happier. But there I
was, wanting more than anything for you to be a part of the
dream I was building while ignoring what you really wanted.

I didn't know what that was, because I didn't ask.

That was the most important thing I should have done; I
didn't do it.

I tell you this with humility and sorrow. It has taken me
many years to unravel this. I will keep picking at it until I
know I have revealed—to myself as much as to you—the
depths of the trauma I have faced. I cannot be afraid of that
yard where the great magnet picks up lives and drops them
into some kind of crushing machine.

Dad

Freedom Is Writing Your Own Narrative

Dear Sekou,

In this letter I want to talk about how to create your own universe, your own narrative, your own sense of purpose and solidity in the world that will try to force you into being someone you don't want to be. Everyone faces this pressure at some point in their lives, but I already see in you a force, a sense of self, a containment, that if you nurture it will keep you safe from the storms of other people's opinions. Some people are put onto this planet to change it, and I see in you a boy who affects everything around him. The quiet, private, uninvolved life is not for you. You're going to have a big effect upon the world, but to do so, you have to gain control of who you are and what you offer.

When I was released from prison in 2010, a year and a half before you were born, a lot of people urged me to remain silent about my past. I was told to simply get a job at a gas station or a fast-food joint and go about my life, keeping my head down and hiding from the things I'd done. In telling me to hide, they were in essence telling me to wait for someone else to tell me when it was okay to be me. I could have followed their advice, for sure; working in a gas station or slinging burgers for a living might have been the easier route, given everything I'd been through. But I chose differently, for a few reasons.

First, I knew that I could never be fully present to myself without addressing my past. Second, I couldn't have avoided that past even if I'd tried. On every job or housing application I filled out, I was asked if I had been convicted of a crime. To so many people, I was not someone who had committed murder twenty years before; I was a murderer and always would be. I was physically and emotionally a completely different person—hell, I no longer even had the same *cells* as that nineteen-year-old boy—but that mark would remain on me forever, it seemed.

Today, I'm fortysomething years old. I'm a father, a tech executive in a C-suite. I collect sneakers. I mentor kids across the country. Yet I still find myself wanting to shout to the world, "This is who I am today!" I am not that boy with the gun in his hand.

Back then, a lot of my friends were still in prison, and I knew that no matter what I did in my own life, I would never be truly free if I forgot about the men I'd left behind. We'd grown up together, shared our lives for two decades, been through so many of the same things in prison. Sometimes we didn't even need to communicate; we just knew what it felt like to be treated as less than human. Those men had become my friends, and friends don't leave friends behind. It's the same attachment military veterans feel toward their units.

On the day I left prison, a guard told me he expected to see me back in six months; he said it casually, as though nothing I could possibly do would change the course of my postin- carceration life.

That was a decade ago.

But even though I took a risk and decided to speak publicly about my story, I still find myself fighting a daily battle to write a true and real narrative that honors all of who I am. There is the public me, and then there is the private me, with all his secret moments of struggle. It's not easy to translate such a life onto the page, to speak honestly and fully about it. You must affirm yourself daily; otherwise you'll be pushed and pulled as though you're in constant bad weather. You need to find the peace inside yourself that comes from knowing who you are and what you stand for and what you want to show to the world.

I was lucky that I didn't have to fight those fights alone. In the years since my release, I've found community among countless people who are also fighting to change the criminal justice system.

By 2015, five years after I'd been released, the conversation around criminal justice was heating up. In her book *The New Jim Crow: Mass Incarceration in the Age of Colorblindness*, the brilliant Michelle Alexander had put the world on notice that the criminal justice system was reintroducing racist laws and a new version of slavery to Black and Brown communities. I was being called on more and more to speak out about the inhumanity of the system.

Through my work with BMe, a network of leaders that

invests in Black men throughout the United States, men who usually struggle to get enough funding to do the work to enhance the quality of life in their communities, I met MIT Media Lab director Joi Ito. He and I had become close friends, to the point where I often stayed at his home when I was in Boston. We spent many late evenings discussing the injustices taking place in our judicial system, including the death of Aaron Swartz. Aaron was a young tech prodigy who had committed suicide after being indicted for downloading academic journal articles illegally and other crimes, which carried a sentence of up to thirty-five years in prison and $1 million in fines. I recall sitting up late at night with Joi discussing how messed up the system was to steal a young life like Aaron's and what we could do about it. We didn't know quite what to do, but we knew that together we could find the right people to help us figure it out.

During a conversation with Joi, I decided to write my memoir, *Writing My Wrongs: Life, Death, and Redemption in an American Prison,* because I felt the conversation had become so academic that the human element had all but been erased. There were facts and figures, but what of the daily lived experience across two decades—what was each moment like, what were the feelings like? How much, in short, did it cost? I self-published my memoir and began hustling copies out of the trunk of my car. Slowly, requests for me to speak about my prison experience began to pick up. Within months of publishing my memoir I had become a public figure, speaking to crowds, telling my story over and over.

By the end of the year, I had been extended an invitation to teach at the University of Michigan by Professor Ashley

Lucas. We had met in prison during a Prison Creative Arts Project theater workshop. Students who enrolled in the class got to make theater, do creative writing, and attend visual arts workshops. There was also a yearly art exhibit featuring work by incarcerated men and women. Those workshops were an incredible lifeline; they offered us a creative outlet and an opportunity to connect with artists in the free world.

When I met Ashley in prison, I just knew that we would find a way to collaborate when I was released. Several years later, it happened. Professor Lucas and I co-founded and taught a course called "The Atonement Project," based on an arts- and tech-based project I had started as part of my fellowship at MIT Media Lab. We were later nominated for a TED Prize, a million-dollar award (which I clearly didn't win). But the nomination reflected the reality that people were ready to have meaningful conversations about criminal justice reform, and we ended up becoming one of twenty global finalists—all after being told that I would be back in prison in six months.

That all came about because I was determined to write my own story, create my own narrative, and not wait for the world outside prison to accept me or open doors for me. I already knew that the world didn't work that way. We were on a trash heap; nothing was expected of us. I wanted so passionately to change the story, to show that I was alive, fully human, and ready to take my place.

Soon, Joi had brought a new person into my orbit, but I couldn't imagine why at first.

When Joi first introduced me to the CNN host and

contributor Van Jones, I thought Joi was crazy to think we'd be friends and collaborators. Van and I couldn't have been more different. On the surface, Van seemed like a straitlaced, if eloquent, nerd. He wore tailored suits and wire-rimmed glasses and had a clean-shaven head and a neatly trimmed mustache. I wore loose street apparel and fashionable sneakers, with a ubiquitous Detroit Tigers hat covering a head full of locks. Van's interviews were polished, professional, and eloquent, while mine were straightforward, raw, and jagged around the edges. But as soon as we connected, all those differences disappeared; I realized immediately that Van was genuine, thoughtful, and razor sharp. His passion for justice and equality leapt through the phone as we talked in depth about the state of Black people and where we were headed as a country.

We talked for nearly two hours, and by the end of our call I felt as though we had known each other for years. We discussed fatherhood, the experience of being a Black man in America, police brutality, and what we could do together to change the systems that were threatening to rip the country apart. I was impressed by Van's intelligence and deep spiritual values. He was impressed, I like to think, by my resilience and my refusal to let my past cloud my hopeful vision for the future.

When our call ended, I felt as though something divine had happened.

Several months later, I ran into Van at a conference in Dallas. I was having dinner in the lobby with a group of my fellows whom I had met through a fellowship with the Kellogg

Foundation. (They were an amazing group of women turned friends whom I later dubbed "The Queens.") We were three drinks in, talking about our work in Michigan and how it connected to larger issues, when Van walked in. I went and greeted him and asked if he had a moment to join us. He kindly accepted, but I didn't know back then that Van didn't drink, and I am sure we were probably a bit obnoxious, considering that we had been engrossed in what we called our "drunken wisdom circle." Van was gracious with his time, though, and eventually he and I were able to talk privately about our work.

Van told me about an organization called #cut50, a bipartisan group brought together to work out how to reduce both crime and incarceration across all fifty states. At the time, he was just getting it off the ground. His co-founder and the executive director of #cut50 was an amazing woman named Jessica Jackson whom Van described as one of the most kickass humans he had ever met. Once I met Jessica, I understood immediately why he had characterized her that way. Southern born and molded in the fires of the injustice system, she had gone back to college to become a lawyer after her husband had received an excessive prison sentence. She was ready to change the world, even if she had to do it alone. Unbeknown to me, she had already seen a talk I'd given, and she wanted to collaborate. It was easy for me to join their efforts, but even so, Van leapt out of his seat and let out a yelp when I agreed to be part of his and Jessica's work. (That yelp is something we joke about to this day.)

All these years and many battles later, we are still at war against a justice system that seeks to destroy communities rather than build them. Jessica, Matt Haney (another co-founder), and Van were all way smarter than I will ever be politically. They understood how to work with politicians from across the aisle, and their legal training helped them navigate how to create workable policies. Yet I felt that I had something to add to the team.

That proved to be true about a year later, when we hosted the largest bipartisan summit on criminal justice in the country's history. We initially thought we would start with twenty or so people from both parties. We ended up with close to eight hundred.

The entire team worked around the clock connecting with governors, senators, and stakeholders who were advocating for justice. The team even secured an exclusive interview between President Barack Obama and the writer David Simon to discuss the brokenness of our prison system. Jessica and I joked with the Secret Service as we welcomed politicians from both parties, press representatives, and criminal justice advocates to the conference.

In a matter of weeks, we had gone from talking about changing the system to actually starting to do it, there at the highest levels of power. Later in the day, Van called us up to speak after President Obama's interview with David Simon had ended. Jessica and I looked at each other and said, "No pressure"—after all, we were only speaking after the most popular man in the world outside of Michael Jordan. To cap it all off, not long after the summit we were invited to the White House, on September 18, 2015.

★　★　★

Think about this, my dear son. I had been let out of prison in 2010 and told that I'd be back in six months. Now I was slated to go to the White House just five years later. For a brief second, I thought of the guard who'd said I'd be back, but his prejudice wasn't worth concentrating on. I had overcome his hatred so many times already.

What I could not overcome was the cruel rigidity of the barriers postincarcerated people face every single day.

I would have never imagined that my first visit to the White House would leave me standing outside in the sweltering Washington, D.C., heat, embarrassed and disappointed. At the time there was a policy barring people with violent felonies from the place, so when I showed up for the event, I was politely but firmly denied entrance. We were at a security booth by a side entrance to the building, and people stared at me awkwardly as they walked past. All I could think about was how I was sure they could see the big scarlet letter F, for Felon, emblazoned on my sweaty forehead. How dare this felon think he is worthy of walking into the White House? I imagined they thought. My heart was like a rock in my chest; I truly felt like shit.

Out there in the swelter I was texting back and forth with Nisha Anand and Alex Gudich from our #cut50 team; they were feverishly working to help me gain access while doing their best to keep me calm. Meanwhile, no matter how much I encouraged him to go ahead without me, Matt Haney refused to go inside; instead, he stood by my side.

That was a true friend.

Van was inside delivering his remarks on a panel hosted

by Angie Martinez, a musician and host at New York's Power
105.1 FM radio station. When Van finished speaking, White
House officials finally sent several staff members outside to
get me. As soon as I walked into the room, everyone stared
at me. I'd been kept outside for so long in the hot sun that I
was sweating profusely, but my discomfort cracked when the
room broke into applause and hoots and hollers.

Van took me to a quieter area where people were waiting
to go into the back to meet the president, and when he left,
I realized I was alone with Angie Martinez. She is one of my
absolute favorite hip-hop personalities, but I knew I couldn't
fanboy out—this was the White House, and your father was
trying to stay cool. But I knew I had to say something, so I
asked her to tell me the most interesting thing that she had
experienced that day.

"I was moderating a panel," she said, "when Van Jones
started to talk about this guy named Shaka—"

"Oh, that's me," I said.

Angie looked at me with tears in her eyes and gave me a
big hug, but our conversation was cut short when she was
called in to meet with President Obama. I felt naked and alone
standing there, waiting for my turn to meet the president.
But I had come this far, and I managed to relish the moment.
After my first parole denial in late 2008, the hope Obama
spoke about in his campaign had sustained me through the
storm of delayed freedom. His resilience and grace under fire
were keys to leadership I had incorporated into my life. My
mind ran across all the ways the interaction might go: Would
the president be cordial, or would he be curious, as so many
others were?

But before I could meet him, he was called to the podium to give his remarks. I went and took a seat in the front row to listen. He talked about his experience of being the first sitting president to go inside a prison and how he believed everyone deserved a second chance. It was surreal sitting there listening to the United States' president talking about men and women who had had experiences similar to mine. "I had second chances," he said. "In some cases, I had resources or I was in an environment in which when I made a mistake as a teen, that I could recover from it. And these young people didn't have any margin for error."

I was moved by Obama's words. I, too, believe that humans are redeemable and that we as a society can get justice only when we are willing to give second chances to those who make mistakes. Soon he was gone, and I left, too, excited to think that my work was helping people see the full humanity of incarcerated women and men. I hadn't met him, but I had made it to the White House, pressing the case for a fairer world for people who had been in prison. That was enough for now.

Six months later, on March 31, 2016, we were invited back. That time I breezed through security. I was later told that the policy had been changed based on my experience the first time. I have no idea if that's true or not, but I'll take it.

For the second time in a year, I came just short of meeting President Obama. (By the time I arrived, he'd been called away on presidential business.) It was a bit of a letdown, but I salvaged what would otherwise have been a disappointing visit by photobombing the White House with pictures of my memoir. I put the book all around the place and took a load of photos of it. That was a small part of my legacy for you, Sekou: your father had taken his work to the center of the country's political life and had created a memorial of it, right there amid the paintings and the flowers and the hallways where so many important people had trodden. Who goes from living in the big house to photobombing the White House in a matter of six years? Your dad, that's who. I wanted you to see what was possible; from the deepest depths I had come up for air in a place where power resides.

There was another reason I photobombed the place. I knew that the White House would never be the same once the Obamas left. By some deep instinct, I knew it was my only chance to commemorate my experience by running amok in the place.

But I still hadn't met the guy. Here was the most powerful Black man in the world, and it would mean so much for me to engage him in conversation. I knew I stood for so many incarcerated and formerly incarcerated people. I wasn't quite ready to give up hope. Our judicial system isn't set up for men and women to return to society healthy and whole. We are expected to fail—urged to do so, in fact—and for all the political will in the world (and there isn't much of it), it remains so hard to create a positive life after prison. But I wasn't going to be disheartened by that day. I was still a firm believer that positive thinking attracts positive outcomes, so I continued to think about what the first handshake with the first Black president would be like.

Nearly a year later, I would finally find out.

★ ★ ★

In February 2017, just shy of a year since *Writing My Wrongs* had come out, I was helping my publishers prepare a marketing strategy for the paperback edition. The hardcover had appeared on the *New York Times* bestseller list—imagine that, Sekou. When I got the call from my agent telling me the news, I felt outside of myself. I'd written in my journal years earlier about the things I wanted to achieve as a writer. Holy shit, I thought—that dream was now real. I felt validated; not only did my words matter, my life mattered, too.

My good friend Felicia Horowitz was one of the first people I reached out to for help with the new edition of the book. She helped me curate a list of guests for a party Sheryl Sandberg had agreed to host. As the RSVPs came in, I learned that Felicia's husband, Ben Horowitz, a technology entrepreneur and venture capitalist, had been scheduled to have dinner with President Obama the evening of the party but had canceled his meeting with the president of the United States so that he could celebrate my book. It was such an honor and an act of extraordinary friendship. These are the moments you should look out for in your life—when someone gives up something important to love on you.

The morning after the party, I went with Ben and Felicia to attend a talk he was giving. En route we stopped at an undisclosed location where Ben and Felicia were to meet Valerie Jarrett, a senior adviser to President Obama. As I waited outside, Felicia texted me to come join them. We walked briskly down a long hallway, and when I turned a corner, there was President Obama. He was taller than I'd imagined, and he broke out into his trademark huge smile. We exchanged the universally understood "Black nod," which Black people who don't know each other but know each other always share.

"So I heard you got a book," he said.

"Yes, Mr. President," I said. "That is true. Unfortunately, I don't have one with me today." (Of course, secretly I was kicking myself because I didn't actually have a copy on me— for about the only time ever!)

"Oh, so the president can't get a copy?" he said, laughing.

Felicia and Ben had told him a bit about my journey and my work in criminal justice reform, and he thanked me for my service. Our meeting over, as I walked away, I couldn't help but wonder how a nineteen-year-old convicted murderer had just that moment, free and forty-five years old, shaken the hand of the forty-fifth president. Here, now, a circle had been completed. I had conceived of a new way, had created a new narrative, and the president was thanking me for the hope I was giving to those still left behind.

Hope is one of the things that I believe we underestimate. Whether we give it or receive it, it remains one of the most sustainable emotional gifts of the human spirit. Obama offered hope to several generations through his words and courage in the face of adversity and doubt. He never shrank himself based on his race or his upbringing. When I think of the "dream" Dr. Martin Luther King, Jr., described in his most famous speech, I can't help but think that it looks something like former president Barack Obama and first lady Michelle Obama. I also can't help but think that it looks something like working alongside Van, Matt Haney, Jessica Jackson, and many others who strive tirelessly to improve lives in real ways every day.

This is the hope I bequeath you, my son. Hatred is everywhere and always will be, but there's one thing that can defeat hatred, and that's hope. When you write your own narrative, write it from a place of hope; fill it with optimism and opportunity and a sense that everything is possible. Don't think of roads that dead-end. Think of endless tracks across a beautiful space, like a spaceship heading out into who knows what. Hope is not some vague, soft-focus dream; it's a muscular, powerful antidote to hate.

Think of your own father's life: I went from a cruel guard telling me he'd see me in six months to the handshake I received from the president. Just make sure that when you've published your book, you keep a copy in your back pocket at all times. You never know who may want one.

Dad

Parenting

Dear Sekou,

I'm writing to you about the two people who have tried to love you more passionately and more deeply than anyone on the planet: your mother and father. I want to tell you what we've learned about you, about each other, and about how to be parents, together and apart.

I'm sorry your mother and I were not able to stay together in the traditional sense of a nuclear family—but I'm also not sorry, and this letter will attempt to explain to you why I can feel two things at the same time. It's a good lesson to learn. It's easy to think that you have to come down on one side or another of an issue when in fact, real strength comes in being able to see all parts of the puzzle.

For many people, being in a nuclear family— mother and father and children all living in the same place, the relationship of the parents intact—is the be-all and end-all of what is considered "normal." And for many people, "normal" is the ultimate thing to strive for. You've seen this in school, for example: kids who are "different" can be picked on or worse; no one wants to stand out; no one wants to be considered "other." And the nuclear family seems so normal. It's the way of biology and history, two people joining together to raise a child in the same home.

Your experience has been different, of course, ever since you've been able to remember. You were three when your mother and I could no longer stay together in a romantic relationship. Your mother has spoken about how hard the breakup was, and I felt it deeply, too. I had come out of prison with great hopes for the future of that relationship, but it was not to be. We found ourselves in the place so many find themselves when a relationship breaks up—working through our anger and resentment, negotiating custody issues and child support—while still focusing on loving you the best we could. Most important, though, was that you were taken care of and raised in a place of love and safety and positivity. Both your mother and I had longed for safety and positivity when we were children, and too often they had been luxuries we just could not locate.

Your mother has spoken openly about the violence she experienced as a child. When your mother was twelve years old, her father held a pistol to her mother's head; your Gigi pleaded with that man and managed to break free before he fired. But though the bullet missed, your mother's family was never the same; your mother would never be the same, either. It was hard for her to trust her parents, so she hid in her books and in her education. But she's resilient, and she decided to make sure that when she was old enough to raise a child, the experience would be different, so different; and so it has been.

In my case, the end of our family as I'd known it came in 1983. I remember it as though it were yesterday. I was eleven years old, standing with my father in the basement of our home on the east side of Detroit. Tears ran down his face as he stuffed albums into bright blue and orange milk crates. Just moments earlier he and my mother had sat my siblings and me down to inform us that they were separating and calling it quits. It still hurts, all these years later.

Thirty years on, tears ran down my face as I packed my own belongings, just like my father. I couldn't believe your mother and I were calling it quits.

When she and I met, I was on year fifteen of my nineteen-year prison sentence. The belief your mother had in me, the imagination to see me beyond my situation then, is nothing short of miraculous. She didn't meet the writer, the activist, the guy with the *New York Times* bestseller. She met a guy fresh out of solitary, a guy with a murder conviction who was still so traumatized by what had happened in his life, a man in the midst of nineteen years of incarceration, much of it in solitary confinement. I was angry and hurt. Some days I couldn't see the future; it was like a gray light in a gray sky. Nevertheless, your mother saw something in me that I maybe hadn't even fully seen in myself by that point—a capacity to love. I truly don't know how she saw it. What she did takes an incredible belief in humanity, and in possibility, in care, and love. All the things that she and I have tried to pass on to you.

This is how we did it: For four years, we wrote letters,

shared phone calls and visits, and did whatever we could to help build an unshakable bond, one that would endure the rigors of life on the outside. Those were our lifelines. Together we battled the system, a system that put me in solitary without cause and denied my parole two years in a row. She was a poet, a dreamer, a visionary. She was beautiful, with a PhD; I was handsome, with a GED. We started a company together and made big plans to live the happiest life possible. It was the love story dreams are made of. Together we believed that we could right the wrongs of our parents, and I could be the father I had always hoped I could be.

Eventually I was released. Now our relationship was conducted out in a world that was new and foreign to me, and old and familiar to her. We were two people connecting in a time warp, a place where the past and the future collided in an almost unreal present. We spent every waking moment together; buying groceries, clothes, stuff for the house—the mundane things that seem exciting in the beginning that quickly turn routine. I had to adjust to sleeping in a bed with your mother alongside me; some nights I woke up in a deep sweat, a deep panic, before drifting back off to sleep knowing I was no longer in a cell. There were so many new things for me to learn and appreciate. I spent the first few weeks being tutored by your mother about the modern world I now lived in. Your mother helped me expand my palate beyond the hamburgers and chicken wings I'd mostly consumed since I came home. I even had to relearn how to drive; she went with me when I had my first driver's test. She had to bear with me as I worked out how to be comfortable in public spaces. In a way, your mother was as much my guardian as my romantic partner. I had spent two decades in a cave; your mother had always lived free in a world that trundled along as normal, a place in which changes came organically, not all in a rush once the doors of a prison swung shut.

When you were born, our lives became centered around you, our beautiful boy. I remember when we first brought you home—it was the best feeling in my life. Your mother and I worked together, collaborated, supported each other. She took the morning shift; I took nights. It was the most magical time.

And then it all changed. I knew your mother was planning to go back to work, but I'd been subconsciously avoiding the reality of it in my mind. One morning she came in really excited. "Today's the day!" she said. "Aren't you excited that you and Sekou will be able to build a bond?" I tried to feel it, saying "Yes, I'm ecstatic! I couldn't be more delighted." In my mind, though, a different narrative was playing out: Why in the world would she believe I am capable of caring for a whole baby? Doesn't she realize I drive around the neighborhood in an old-school Chevy all day blaring trap music? I'm basically a kid. I tried to be positive, but inside I was really afraid. I couldn't tell your mother that, so instead I said, "Hey, go off and have a dope day."

And I was left with you, Sekou, and I was terrified—a thirty-eight-year-old child in charge of a baby. I can see now that your mother was trying to foster the trust that's necessary for parents to coexist—she was trusting me with our most precious gift, and she was trying to help me build the foundation for what's important in this portal we call parenthood. But no, I wasn't ready; and yes, I was afraid.

By the time you were three, our relationship had become

unhinged. There were lots of reasons: post-traumatic stress disorder from my brutal incarceration; the damage done in my time before I went to prison, a different but real kind of PTSD; baggage from your mother's previous relationships; my inexperience in any kind of adult romantic relationship—all these things undid the magic of what we'd built behind the walls of a prison. Sometimes freedom is the hardest thing to navigate, especially if you haven't known it as an adult.

The loving relationship we had built was now being dismantled bit by bit and word by word. We argued often—we said mean things, things we could never take back. We behaved as well as we could in your presence, but the poisonous things we said in private could never be unsaid.

But even though our romantic relationship broke, we never wavered in our love for you, Sekou. In fact, we are proud of the parenting we've done. We see it now as an allegory about the two-sided coin of what's possible and what's not possible for Black people in America.

On one side, your mother and I have to face the reality of raising a Black boy in a society that says that Black boys, Black bodies, and Black lives can only be seen as profitable or disposable. We see that everywhere we look—there are just a few things you're allowed to be according to the bullshit media. As far back as I can remember, the depiction of Black males in the media and on TV has been that of a thug or a rogue. The best we could hope for—and what kind of best is this?—was that we'd be cast as the Black police chief giving the two white cops twenty-four hours to once again become the heroes and solve the case. Rarely do we see Black heroes who aren't adorned in basketball, football, or baseball jerseys.

Nor do we see the everyday heroes—the Black fathers who are just doing their best to get by in America. Luckily, during the mid-eighties we started to see a bit of a shift with shows like *The Cosby Show* and *Family Matters,* which depicted professional, educated Black people. But even then, they were the exception to the rule. Today we're starting to see more representation, though we have a long way to go.

We have to be careful of these one-dimensional narratives. We're not monolithic. You can be an athlete who's also an entrepreneur, a rapper who's a businessman. You can be Nas, who raps and is also an investor in Ring. You can be Maurice Ashley, the first Black chess grandmaster. You could be Neil deGrasse Tyson. You can be an accountant if you really like spreadsheets that much. You can be you, whatever that turns out to be.

Your mother and I wanted to raise a boy to be free to be whatever he wants to be, just as boys from the privileged part of America take as their birthright. It's what we have wanted for you from the beginning, Sekou, and so we work toward that. We have created a space for healing, transformation, intimacy, and the possibilities of a world in which parents who are no longer together can openly show one another affection, support, caring, and love publicly, in a way that honors the relationship we have with you. Even more important, we need to be the power that supports each other in all those vulnerable moments, so that you grow up knowing that even if your parents don't live together, their greatest moments in tandem and apart are with you. This can be true for all parents whose relationships have faltered. When the adults disagree, they can work things out themselves in private; but the children must be sanctified by no wavering of love, no outward signs of distress.

Co-parenting is not only a choice that honors what's best for us, it's a choice that honors the best of who we are as parents. We don't always have the answers, but we know that we can always count on each other. We talk often about the things that we know will impact your life; we check in with each other about your feelings; we inform each other about doctor visits and school meetings; on occasion, we just spend time together with you. And we never bad-mouth each other in front of you. We even conspired to surprise you on your ninth birthday with a business all your own (your own affirmational T-shirt line!), one that we invested in equally. All of this requires more than just co-parenting; it is a dedicated partnership that focuses on your happiness, not on our own.

Here's one of those moments when co-parenting works for us. One day, I came to pick you up from school—you were in first grade. As I was waiting, another parent walked up to me and excitedly said, "Hey, Shaka, I saw Oprah Winfrey give a shout-out to you on CNN last night." I was mortified, because I could already imagine that she'd tell another parent who'd tell another parent and then they'd look me up and discover that I had been in prison for murder. And then a child of one of those parents would overhear the conversation and they would, as children can do, come to school and bully you with that knowledge. It was almost too upsetting to bear, so I knew that I had to call your mother. She just said, "You have to have the talk." I agreed and told her I would record it for her, so she could fill in any gaps if necessary. I took you home that day, and as you were getting ready for bed that night, we talked for half an hour—remember? I told you about why I had gone to prison and I listened to what you said. It was one of the hardest but most important conversations I have ever had.

Eventually, we called your mom so we could do our nightly ritual—she offers her prayers, and we do our affirmations. As your parents, we wanted you to know you are powerful, thoughtful, kind, and magical, despite what you might hear when you returned to school the following day. So that night after school and our difficult conversation—and every night—we intoned together, "I'm great. I'm awesome. I'm amazing. I'm thoughtful. I'm loving. I'm caring. I'm funny. I'm smart. I'm a big boy. I'm a warrior. I am Sekou."

Yes, you are Sekou, the great fulfillment of a dream I never knew I could hope for. I'm so proud to be your dad and a coparent with Ebony. Though things didn't go as envisioned between your mother and me, we are fortunate to be building this life for you together. Things don't always need to go according to plan to end up beautifully.

Dad

Stop Resisting

Dear Sekou,

I'm writing this letter to you as our country burns.
Once again, a string of assaults—both physical and
verbal—has been made upon us by a culture that
does not see us as fully human. We are just the latest
generation to be reminded, brutally, that we are in
chains. Our culture does not believe we are worthy
of real freedom because it does not see us as fully
human, to the point where we can be threatened,
screamed at, assaulted, falsely arrested or falsely
imprisoned, and killed, for one reason and one reason alone: we are Black.

New atrocities hit us every day, week, month,
and year, and it can be too easy to forget the details
of what has happened as this rolling, endless litany
of assaults piles onto our backs day after day. So let
me make a memorial of just four incidents in the
last two months. What is striking about these four

incidents is that they only partially show the range of what you might face as you grow up.

On February 23, 2020, a young Black man, Ahmaud Arbery, was jogging in a Georgia neighborhood when two white men—one, a former Georgia cop—decided to chase him down in a truck and shoot him dead. A third white man filmed the murder and was subsequently alleged to have been involved. Let's be clear, my dear son: Arbery was jogging. He wasn't, as those racists alleged, a suspect in neighborhood robberies, nor was he stealing anything from a nearby building site. He was jogging, as he often did in the neighborhood in which he lived. For that, he was murdered.

Then, on March 13, 2020, Breonna Taylor, a twenty-six-year-old Black EMT professional working hard in our pandemic, was asleep in bed in Louisville, Kentucky, when a gang of plainclothes drug cops broke into her home allegedly looking for a suspected drug dealer who was already in custody elsewhere. When Breonna's partner fired a shot in self-defense, the police indiscriminately unloaded twenty rounds, eight of which hit Breonna, killing her. Words like "suspects" were used to describe Breonna and her partner. It wasn't until civil rights activists got involved that the narrative changed, but it will always be too late for Breonna Taylor. She was asleep; she was murdered for being asleep.

Later, there were two separate incidents on the same day, May 25. One showed the toxicity of white privilege, and the other showed the violence that privilege believes is its right.

First, a Black man, Christian Cooper, was enjoying a nature walk in an area of Central Park in New York City called the Ramble when he asked a white woman, Amy Cooper (no relation), to leash her dog. His request was fair; the Ramble is not an area where dogs are allowed off leash, and her dog was threatening the birds Christian wanted to look at. If you can imagine a gentler pastime than bird-watching, well, good luck—but even in the most peaceful of moments, white privilege sees threat: Amy Cooper, incensed by Christian's reasonable request, called 911 and pretended that her life was in danger. "There is a man, African American, . . . threatening me and my dog," she told the dispatcher.

That phone call was an invitation to have police officers kill Mr. Cooper. Nothing more, nothing less. Whether or not she knew that overtly, she certainly knew it at a genetic level—just as Carolyn Bryant in Money, Mississippi, had known it in 1955 when she made the false claims that got Emmett Till lynched.

Then, a few hours after the Christian Cooper assault, a white police officer arrested a Black man, George Floyd, a thousand miles away in Minneapolis. During the arrest, an officer named Derek Chauvin held his knee violently on George's neck for more than nine minutes, killing him while three of his colleagues stood nearby. Since the video of that murder went viral, the country has erupted in frustration and anger. People have taken to the streets to protest, but let's pause for a moment to remember: in the weeks before George's murder, heavily armed white men and women took to the streets across the country to protest the stay-at-home orders during the pandemic. They were allowed to protest as they pleased, with minimal police oversight. When protests began after the murder of George Floyd, the police response was huge, militarized, and violent. One officer in New York

City told a protester she was a stupid fucking bitch before violently pushing her ten feet across the street to the ground, sending her to the hospital. There have been baton charges, rubber bullets, tear gas, pepper pellets, and curfews—a militarized offensive aimed at terrorizing us once again into silence, into remembering our place.

This is the country in which you're being raised. Black bodies can be murdered, threatened with murder, or assaulted, with impunity. The Black body is not considered fully, or even partially, human. And the key way this is brought home to bear, again and again, is via two simple words: "Stop resisting."

That's what we're always told, the magic phrase that, once uttered, gives officers free rein over their subject. Any movement—*any*—after those two words seems to be a good enough excuse to visit violence upon the person who appears to be, in the words of the officer, resisting. But it extends beyond our interactions with police officers. Black people are expected not to resist in all walks of life. If we argue, we're confrontational. If we stick up for ourselves, we're pushy. The trope of the "angry Black," especially Black women, is pervasive.

We resisted in prison.

In the summer of 1995 at the Michigan Reformatory, there were two prison officers who constantly bullied us and harassed us on the yard. They would steal our possessions, throw us up against a wall, even use choke holds on us. We couldn't abide it any longer, but what could we do? If we'd gone after the two officers, it would have been an excuse for the guards in the towers to start shooting.

Eventually, various organizations—gang leaders and religious leaders and everyday guys—held meetings to decide what we'd do about the men. Most believed that the only way to fix the issue was to be violent. But that would have gotten us nowhere, except maybe dead on the yard ourselves.

Instead, we examined the prison rules. We were allowed to meet in groups of six and no more to exercise, but it didn't say how many groups of six were allowed. So what we did was to organize the entire yard—three hundred men—into groups of six. Each group did a different workout exercise but counted at exactly the same cadence. Imagine that, fifty groups of six, all working out at the same time in different disciplines but to the same call. I can only imagine how terrifying it looked; it was not how days on the yard usually went. Time on the yard was not organized. Normally there were ragtag groups playing basketball, playing cards, going back and forth to the store, or making phone calls home. We were not *supposed* to organize or be unified, and by doing so, we were signaling that we could take over the prison if we wanted to.

Our actions that day froze the prison. Officers came rushing out and down from the gun tower, thinking it was the start of a riot or a rebellion. Then, just as quickly as we had assembled, we disassembled, going back to a throng of men.

Our message was heard. Though a few of us were taken to segregation and some to the warden's office, and some were even transferred to another prison, we had made our point.

I have been asked many times whether or not I'll join the protests currently happening in our country. I protested in Detroit after an attendant at a gas station killed a man who had questioned him over the price of condoms, of all things. I took you to those uprisings. But now, with people being arrested and hit with batons, to join in on the streets now I would be putting my freedom at risk. I already have two felonies; a third would put me away forever. I know how important this moment is, and I want to take you out. But with such a threat to my freedom, I have to find other ways for us to resist. My task is to give you the right information to prepare for your coming battles.

"Stop resisting." These are the words our culture has for Black boys, men, and women when we are simply trying to breathe, let alone rebel. We are told to stop resisting by cops, yes, but also by more than just cops—by angry white women in Central Park. We are told to stop resisting when protests erupt in the streets. We are told that we must be as peaceful as a church service, otherwise our resistance is "violent" or it's going against the memory of George Floyd. We're reminded that property is sacred, even when human lives are not.

Cops use those two words, "Stop resisting," as a kind of magical cloak behind which they feel free to do whatever they wish with the Black body in front of them. They shout the words at those they are arresting for no reason who have the temerity not to acquiesce to an unlawful order. Or they use them as a smoke screen for when a police officer is brutalizing a citizen. What it means is "Hey, I can cause you pain and discomfort first, but if you push back at that in the slightest way, you're resisting, so I then have complete freedom to use your body as I wish." Or "I can threaten your life with a gun or a choke hold or a knee to the neck, and if you don't meekly give in to that pain, then you're resisting, and I can escalate to whatever degree I like." You can be as passive as the officer wants you to be or as passive as a white woman in a park needs you to be, but if you are not cowed by the cloak of power he or she wields—if you are not subdued in the way of the enslaved person—then you are resisting, and they can do whatever they want to you until you stop resisting.

How will a cop know that you've stopped resisting? There's only one way to be truly sure. George Floyd stopped resisting. Walter Scott stopped resisting in South Carolina in 2015 when a cop pulled out a gun and made sure that he could never resist again. Eric Garner stopped resisting on a street in Staten Island when he was pulled to the ground in a choke hold and murdered for the sin of not going along completely with his own abuse. It also happens in prison; innocent Black men on death row are just another brick in the edifice of state-sanctioned murder.

So what am I to tell you, Sekou, if you're told to "stop resisting"? Should you do so? Was Eric Garner resisting when his life was ended by a choke hold? Was George Floyd resisting for the more than nine minutes a cop kept his knee on his neck? Chris Cooper resisted in the most mundane of ways, and his life was thereafter in the balance.

For years, the Black community has dealt with this injustice by "having the talk" with its young men. Even the mayor of New York City—a man who has a Black son and who is in control of the police force—said in 2014, "With Dante, very early on with my son, we said, 'Look, if a police officer stops you, do everything he tells you to do, don't move suddenly, don't reach for your cellphone.' Because we knew, sadly, there's a greater chance it might be misinterpreted

if it was a young man of color." The response by the police
union? Its president said, "If this individual, who's in charge
of running this city, doesn't have faith in his own son being
protected by the NYPD, he may want to think about moving out of New York City completely. He just doesn't belong
here." That's right—a father who dared name the reality of
racism was threatened with being run out of town by his own
police force.

So am I to have this talk with you? Am I to tell you to not
resist so that you might stay alive?

I'm fed up with people asking me what I am going to tell
you to do if you are confronted by police. The reality is that
there is nothing I can tell you to protect you against a racist
cop who is hell-bent on breaking your back, kneeling on your
neck, or choking the life out of you; there's nothing I can tell
you about the slurs you'll hear, the times you'll be followed
or detained or questioned for merely being on a street. So
instead, I must out of necessity teach you how to physically
defend yourself. If you must die—a thought so heartbreaking
I don't want to even write the words—I would rather you
died fighting back, because it is clear to me that complying to
commands to stop resisting will end with you being carried
away in a body bag.

The poet Claude McKay wrote about this very thing in
1919:

IF WE MUST DIE

If we must die, let it be not like hogs
Hunted and penned in an inglorious spot,
While round us bark the mad and hungry dogs,

Making their mock at our accursèd lot.
If we must die, O let us nobly die,
So that our precious blood may not be shed
In vain; then even the monsters we defy
Shall be constrained to honor us though dead!
O kinsmen! we must meet the common foe!
Though far outnumbered let us show us brave,
And for their thousand blows deal one death-blow!
What though before us lies the open grave?
Like men we'll face the murderous, cowardly pack,
Pressed to the wall, dying, but fighting back!

I'm sick of the pickets and protests that haven't stopped the racists of the world from attempting to get us killed or arrested. I'm tired of listening to leaders talk about how we have to hold people accountable. How can we hold people accountable when the system that employs and validates them is corrupt? How can we hold people accountable when a large part of society is indifferent to the suffering of Black boys and men and women? I'm tired of memes and social media posts that allow us to hit a "like" or "share" button to say we have done our part. None of these things makes me feel safe as a Black man, friend, or father in America—in fact, nothing makes me feel safe. I am exhausted, just as our options are exhausted, yet there is a part of me that refuses to give up or give in. Meanwhile I will continue to ask myself tough questions, like: What can I do to make my son and other Black boys feel safe and empowered? What can I do to let them know they are loved? What can I do to eradicate the fear that they will die because of their blackness? What the fuck can I do?

It starts with this: resist. There is a proud history of resistance that you need to learn about and internalize and feed upon when you are called to act. As enslaved people we sabotaged tools, created the music of resistance, fled via the Underground Railroad. We stole our masters' food and liquor and livestock; we fought against the forces of racism in the Civil War and after. We fought back in the Red Summer riots in 1919, in Chicago and Washington, D.C., and elsewhere. We created sit-ins and protests and freedom rides and boycotts throughout the civil rights era. We have been Harriet Tubman and Malcolm X and Rosa Parks and Moses Wright, Emmett Till's great-uncle, who stood up in a court in the deep South in 1955 and pointed to a white man, accusing him of murdering his nephew. In prison we organized resistance, such as the cadence trick in Michigan. We have created Million Man and Woman marches and Black Lives Matter.

This is resistance.

So many men and women have done their part; now it's up to you to do yours. Forget the callout, the cancel, or the shaming culture. This is heart and gut check time. This is a time for us to reimagine collectively what it means to stand for something. This is your moment to exercise a higher way of seeing and believing in the best that is us. This is a moment for clarity of vision, for good people to listen to one another in a spirit of openness. We have people on the front lines and people operating in the back. Their efforts are equally important. Resistance looks different to everyone; all should be honored.

This is a visceral time of reckoning, not only with who we are but with who we can become. Never diminish someone's efforts because they aren't the same as yours. There is no greater than or less than, it all counts. In this moment, and in the future moments when we're called to respond, we have to love up our people to a state of active engagement.

Above all, this is your calling as a young Black man in America: no longer should you not resist, and no longer will I abide by telling you to do so. And no longer will I hold out the expectation that you must wait on the hope that those you deal with will treat you fairly. As Malcolm X said, "I believe in the brotherhood of man, all men, but I don't believe in brotherhood with anybody who doesn't want brotherhood with me. I believe in treating people right, but I'm not going to waste my time trying to treat somebody right who doesn't know how to return that treatment."

I'm tired of talking to you about racism, about my anger at racist culture. As you grow, you'll hear about so-called diversity training and all the other socially and politically correct bullshit words used to soothe our pain. These salves have served no purpose other than to silence our cries and dry our tears. You no longer need to follow these fake hopes toward peace. When faced with confrontation, resist. Resist with passion; resist with a ramrod back; resist with the surety that you are a human being. The first step in resistance is to aver that you are indeed human. Those who lose sight of this truth will seek to deny you due process and fair treatment on the streets and in the courts and will try to jail you whether or not you have committed a crime. Resist; resist the narrative that you are not a boy, that you are not a man, that you are not human.

I'm tired, Sekou—I'm tired of all this. I'm tired because

I know that the list of murders of body and spirit that I put into this letter will already be out of date by next week, next month, next year—perhaps by tomorrow. Somewhere tonight, even, somewhere in America, a racist cop will violently grab a Black person and will hurt him or her physically, will treat him or her as nonhuman, will tell him or her that he or she may not drive, cross the street, walk, or even sleep. That person will have perhaps had the talk with his or her parents, and will know that he or she should acquiesce, but the invisible chains clank and taunt, and the slightest movement—the inability of a human being to ever fully be a statue—will seem like resistance to the culture, and the violence will intensify as the culture screams, "Stop resisting!" And then there is no stopping what will come.

This is the core of what you must become. Resist the world of idiots telling you who you are, what you can be, and how to live. You are a king. Be a king! Show the world that you are untouchable by the expectations and chains others will hurl at you. You are the most extraordinary fluke of genetics, a lucky roll of the cosmic dice, a number that came up that can never come up again. This chance alone should make you a king, should lead you into the strength of your self and the power of your own soul, arrayed against all limitations, all assaults, all reductions and diminutions.

So I'm not too tired to tell you this: resist. Always resist. Resist in the deepest part of you, my king.

With all my love,
Dad

Isolation

Dear Sekou,

I want to talk to you about solitude and isolation. I have known a lot of both in my life. For me, it began early: from having a neighbor attempt to molest me to watching my brothers go off to a boys' home to lying alone in a hospital bed after being shot, I have known what it means to be completely alone. There will be times in your life when you're alone—very alone—and you need to be able to deal with it.

I was in solitary confinement for a large portion of my time in prison. In total it came to about seven years, but there was one stretch when I did four years straight. From October 1999 to March 2004, I woke up every morning inside a six-by-nine-foot solitary confinement cell. For five days a week, for years, I got to leave my cell for only one hour a day (and let's not even think about the prison's policy that kept me in solitary on twenty-four-hour lockdown for two days a week). Isolation is inhumane;

it causes profound damage to human beings. No one leaves there without deep scars; no one.

Many others have written eloquently about isolation and how damaging it can be. Anne Frank, in her famous diary, wrote that one particular day, Sunday, was dreadful to her:

> I wander from one room to the next, down the stairs and back up again and feel like a songbird that has had its wings torn off and flies against the bars of its cage in total darkness. "Outside, fresh air and laughter," a voice inside me screams; I don't even try to answer anymore, I lie down on a divan and sleep in order to shorten the time, the silence, the terrible fear too, because there is no question of killing them.

I understand that so well; a sense that one's very essence, the wings of the songbird, has been lost to the sense of aloneness. And the voices in your head don't just talk when you're isolated—they scream. Reading Anne Frank, it's amazing to think that though our outward experiences were so different and took place at such different times in history, our shared sense of despair makes us siblings in pain. This is what isolation does: it creates a family—no family you'd ever want to be in but a family all the same—gathered around a hearth of torture and fear and a mind in turmoil.

Nelson Mandela was part of that family, too. He spent eighteen years on Robben Island, usually in a cell just eight feet by seven feet. Sometimes he'd be placed in solitary for something as simple as reading newspaper clippings. His times in isolation were as routine as they were without cause.

Twice a year, he was allowed to write one letter and have one visitor. In his autobiography he wrote:

> The authorities believed that isolation was the cure for our defiance and rebelliousness. . . . I found solitary confinement the most forbidding aspect of prison life. There was no end and no beginning; there is only one's own mind, which can begin to play tricks.

The greatest threat of isolation is that your mind can lose its bearings. We forget how interactions with other people and with the natural world around us can work to anchor our imaginations and our thoughts—without those things, we can be set entirely adrift, our minds like albatrosses flying across vast oceans, unable to land to take our bearings.

In solitary I was anxious, stressed out, and deeply depressed. A lot of that had to do with the uncertainty of the situation: I never knew when I was going to be released back into the general prison population, so every time an officer or counselor approached my door, my body would tense up and my palms would sweat. "Is this the day they are going to tell me the nightmare is over?" I'd wonder. I eventually realized that I was trying to control something I had no control over, a labor that only brings more suffering.

Now, you won't ever have to face solitary confinement in a prison, God willing, so you might be wondering why I'm telling you about all this. Well, isolation comes in many forms. For one, we've all suffered through the social distancing of the pandemic. But long after the lockdowns lift, there will be times, even in the best of years, when you'll find yourself very alone. Perhaps you'll be traveling solo; perhaps a relationship you're in will end; perhaps you'll go to college and find it hard to make friends; perhaps you'll be old one day, and your social circle will contract to just a few people. Maybe you'll have countless friends but still feel alone. A lot of people feel that way—surrounded by loved ones but unable to connect, to feel truly seen and understood.

All these things can cause a feeling of isolation, of loneliness, of dislocation. You may feel as though you don't have your feet on the ground; it's like a heavy weightlessness; it feels like being adrift but at the same time sluggish. It's like being anchored by a malignant force you can't see.

This is a dangerous feeling, and I want to draw you a road map out of it.

The first thing to understand is that feelings of isolation become worse if you can't see a way out. For me, that happened every time I was not let back into the general population. I would watch other men get out, or I'd head up to a hearing for release, only to be denied. People told me I would be there forever, and I started to believe it.

Whatever the reason for your isolation, it can leave you feeling as though you'll never love again, you'll never make friends again, the terror you feel now will never subside. But that's the first thing to understand, the great trick of being alive: things change. Nothing stays the same forever. Sometimes we might wish it to, when things are going good. Alas, everything changes, and that's a positive thing. So in those moments of deep isolation, please know that eventually something will come along to change the situation. Remember how I used to think that I'd never get out of solitary? Well, this morning you and I had breakfast together in our house in Los Angeles.

Everything changes.

But you don't have to wait for things to change, either—you can make change happen. I had to learn that the hard way. When I was in isolation in Wayne County Jail, I often found myself listless, without energy. I discovered that my thoughts and my actions were the only two things I could control; and once I understood that, I was better able to stop "watching the cockroaches" and start making progress. Screw when the prison administration was going to release me; my job was to focus my energy on becoming the best version of myself. When I finally understood that, I realized that I could turn my prison cell into a space of enlightenment, creativity, and higher learning. I studied a different subject every hour. I meditated. And for entertainment, I followed the chess games of the men around me. Because we weren't allowed to have chess sets, the men would draw a board on the back of a note-pad and use small pieces of paper as chess pieces, calling out the moves according to the letters and numbers corresponding to the squares.

And I started writing.

None of that was easy, and it took a long time. But I committed to the belief that I would come out on the other side of the pain healthy and whole, and I was able to do it.

One of the first things I did was to keep a journal. I would write on the backs of envelopes, scraps of paper, anything I could get my hands on. Noting down your experiences is the first way—and sometimes the most powerful—to make sense of the world around you and gain a little control over it. Perspective is crucial in all that you do. Take time to dig into your feelings about the events of each day, even if it's just for a few moments. Doing so will help you sort out what's important about what happened, and what you can let go.

When we first moved to Koreatown, at nighttime you and I would talk. Sometimes we'd stand at the windows in your bedroom, which had floor-to-ceiling glass, and just take in the beautiful LA landscape. There were lights everywhere, twinkling dots of energy all the way up to the dark hills.

We would play a game.

"What do you see when you look out the window?" I'd ask you.

"Ralph's," you'd say, or "McDonald's. Stoplights." Then you'd say, "Daddy, what do you see?"

Well, I saw millions of ideas. Somebody had to develop the cement, the screws, the blocks of concrete, the hinges on doors, the clasps on windows, the locks, the light poles, the street signs, the paint for the roads, the little black plastic cap that goes over the valve in a car wheel. So many ideas made real.

And I'd say to you, "You see those people on the corner? Do you think they see what I see? Probably not, right? They're not up here so high. Does that mean that this world doesn't exist? This world exists. They just can't see it." You can see the vastness of anything if you're looking for it.

When I was in prison, I longed for such conversations. When all you have is time to think, your perspective gets bent like a road after an earthquake. It distorts your sense of what is crucial and what is just noise. Things that would otherwise roll off your back can grow into hundred-pound weights. I remember being filled with rage; rage that too often made me feel as though I'd been forgotten.

The first time I sat down to write something in my journal, it felt like an act of meditation. I wrote freely with no editing, no judgment, just words, and felt an overwhelming sense of joy. You know that excitement when you meet a new friend? That was me, meeting myself. Writing gave me energy— sometimes I would do push-ups immediately afterward or even dance—and it gave me a sense of celebration in a terrible place. I would wait till late at night and write standing up by the door, utilizing the merest sliver of light shining through the crack at the edge. I would write when I was angry or sad or even when I allowed a tiny bit of hope to set in.

Answer this: When was the last time you had an honest conversation with yourself or processed that one thing that doesn't seem to go away? If you're honest in your journal, you'll be able to answer that question by saying "Every day." Because a journal doesn't let you hide; it would be like cheating at golf or something. Journaling, like meditating, is a wonderful way of quieting the voices in your head. We all have those nagging voices: questioning who we are, what we stand for, what we want to be—and worse: fixating on things that have gone wrong, people who have let us down, the moments in our lives that hurt so much that we can't let go.

Back in prison, meditating felt like a foreign land. I was nineteen, and let's just say that meditation had not previously been part of my life—in fact, I'm not sure I'd even heard the word up to that point. I knew this much, though: my thoughts were running fast, an endless ticker like the one at the bottom of ESPN or CNN. The loop of thoughts was endless, and I didn't know how to open the door to let the thoughts out.

One day, I got a pamphlet about how meditation could help me cope with my new reality. I sat down with the pamphlet and tried to take in the lessons on how to breathe and how to empty your mind. When I started feeling anxious and the voices in my head became too insistent, I would lie on my bunk and focus on my breathing. I would inhale for a count of five and slowly exhale for a count of five. On the inhale, I tried to bring in a kind of liberating energy, a sense of hope and possibility; on the exhale, I told myself to release all the counterproductive and damaging thoughts. It was hard in the beginning, but the more I did it, the easier it became to bring my mind to a state of stillness.

The key to meditation was to give myself permission to let go of the things I couldn't control—and being locked in solitary, that was pretty much everything. I had to give up the idea that I could have a family or that my friends would be there for me—none of them had been there for me. My mind couldn't compute that I had decades left in that place. So at nineteen, I pretty much believed, *This is it for me.* But once I let those things go and began to understand that the world wasn't against me—or if it was, I couldn't change it—I arrived at a place where those random thoughts were replaced with affirmations. I was letting in the beautiful light and dismissing the muddy things; it was an incredible therapy for me.

In the end, of course, people need people. Humans crave contact, touch, and engagement, and they need to be seen. I was in prison, don't forget, so emails and texts were out of the question; and it wasn't enough to just wait for a phone call a few times a week. I had to do something to forge connections outside those evil walls, so I did what people have been doing since they invented papyrus (and before, if you count cave art): I wrote, and I wrote to people.

Now, given that you're growing up with a little computer in your pocket, you'll probably think I'm some kind of dinosaur for suggesting that you write letters. Go ahead, call me a stegosaurus so we can move on. But letters literally saved my life, Sekou. Saved. My. Life. Because it wasn't just that I forged connections with people outside the prison and beyond my experience—though that in and of itself is one of the best arguments for writing—no, it was more than that. The letters helped me dive into who I was and understand the forces that had led me to do the things I'd done. I used to think I was a bad kid, instead of a kid who'd had bad things happen to him. I also used to think I was worthy only of the negatives my life had given me—but writing helped me see that I was worthy of other things, like fatherhood, love, and success, and one day, freedom. When you force yourself to compose a sentence, you have to have a clear pathway ahead of you. Writing is not just about the sentence structure and the grammar and the spelling; it's about creating a way forward in your mind, creating a sense of purpose, fulfilling a promise to yourself.

Also, think about receiving a letter—is there anything better, truly? When you go to a mailbox and see your name on the outside of an envelope, it's a whole world of magic waiting for you. The moment before you open it and all the questions that come: What will this person say? What will they tell me about themselves and about me? Will they still be angry? Will they forgive? Will they admit they love me, or have they fallen out of love? Will they talk about a tree they saw or a bird or a coyote in a canyon that paused to look? Will there be a joke, a funny story, a little drawing, perhaps?

This is why many days in your lunch box you'll find a note from me. Sometimes I tell you how much I love the details of you—the way you smile, the way you laugh, the way you get so excited over a new pair of sneakers or when your mind hits on a new thing. Other times, I write you to explain more fully something that's come up in a previous conversation. Letters are magical because they can conjure up a world beyond the one you can see. You want to go to the deepest part of the ocean? Space? The Amazon jungle? Letters can magically take you on that journey. After we moved into our new house, you even put one of my lunch box letters on your wall, so that "every time you leave, you can read it."

Letters are magical objects, and I urge you to both send them—lots of them—and ask to receive them. Unlike email or texts or whatever the next technology will be, letters remain; they are solid, like the trees from which the paper they're written on is made. You can look back on them years and years from now and see who you were and who you wanted to be. You'll see more clearly who the person writing to you was back then and who he or she wanted to be. You can write to your younger self or the old man you will one day be, using letters as checkpoints to track your development. Heck, you might even create a great passion: the letters your mother and I shared still crackle with the urgency of passion and love. Even though it didn't work out between us, those letters are proof, unmitigated evidence that a love existed, and it was real, and it made you, Sekou.

I went to prison at nineteen with a murder conviction; I came out decades later a writer. I don't want you to think that the process of that change was easy, but I do think that the isolation I felt led me to move more inward, to stop beating up the world around me, and to focus on what I could do to be a better person. What flowed from that is my writing career, something that has meant everything to me. Now, I don't know if you want to follow me in this; it's not like a bakery or a farm or a dental practice where the kids take over the family business. Writing is a solitary thing, and it's hard, and I don't know if you'll even want to do such a thing. I do know that you love books, and I couldn't be prouder of you for that. Maybe it will lead you one day to try to write your own. Maybe you'll write about your father or your mother or your extended family; maybe you'll write about the world around you, the culture you live in, or the discrimination you face; or maybe you'll write about politics, sports, or music. The world is open to you in ways that it wasn't for me when I was your age. When I was a kid, Black children didn't have voices; it was better to be seen than heard. Now you're privileged to have a household that considers your presence as sacred. We adore your voice.

I happen to think that everyone should and can write a book. It doesn't have to be published. It's funny: unlike weekend painters, everyone who writes a book thinks it deserves to be in bookstores. But writing a book should be about the process, the effort of thought and construction in the service of honesty. No one has the one truth; but trying to write your truth is the greatest gift you can give yourself. It doesn't necessarily need to be available in bookstores. Maybe it's just for you.

That would be enough.

The key thing about writing, though, be it a letter, a journal, or a book, is this: Be kind to yourself, and give yourself permission to be imperfect. The most important thing is getting that story out of your head and onto paper; it's not about bigging yourself up, letting yourself off, or performing for a crowd. You have to write to work out who you are. So many of us have no idea who we are, and the truth is that most of us are much harder on ourselves than we would ever be on someone else. We forgive others so much quicker than we forgive our own missteps. When you use writing as a tool to see yourself as others might, you'll be amazed at what you find.

Sometimes in isolation, these inner efforts—meditating, journaling, writing—are all well and good, but you also need to remember to do things with your body as well as your mind. By body I mean external things, things that externalize your inner process, things that get your actual blood flowing: running around the yard with your puppy, going on a walk, building something with your hands. Isolation and depression are bunkmates, trust me. And one of the best ways out of depression is to move through time and space.

Serving time in solitary wasn't easy. It was one of the hardest things I've ever endured. There were days when the ghost of the past and the uncertainty of the future threatened to crush the little bit of hope I had of ever being free. But I knew if I could get through the pain of those moments, I could come out on the other side.

I can't promise that you will go through life unscathed. You will lose loved ones, you will have your heart broken, you will break someone's heart. You will have money, and you will lose it; you will have friends, and they will move away. But remember, my son: Each moment is all you really have. Even in isolation, each moment is new and dear and never to come again. Look inside every moment for its brilliance and shine. It's there; you just have to look.

Yours,
Daddy

Decision Making

Dear Sekou,

Conventional wisdom says you should never buy a house when you've just quit your job and started a business that you have no idea will work or not and the world is on the verge of a global pandemic.

But I did it anyway; I bet on myself. Miraculously, that house is now our home. And although that business no longer exists in the way that I'd originally conceived it, I didn't need it—we're doing fine. Sometimes what looks like a decision is actually a miracle, and oftentimes miracles are born out of the decisions we make.

If the world ever wonders if miracles can happen, all it needs to do is look at your hands: magical they are, especially when I hold them in mine or when they write your name or wash your face or lie sweetly beside you as you sleep. I want my love to not only fill your heart but also help you navigate the complexities of the world into which you were unwillingly born. I made so many poor decisions in my childhood—often as the result of trauma. I have been thinking a lot about those decisions.

Making the right choices is a lot harder than picking A or B or C—and picking the right path is one of the most important things you can ever do. It's not easy; I've learned from my bad decisions, and no doubt I'll make some more going forward—everyone does. That's just part of being alive. But I do wish someone had helped me make better decisions before I brought down a rain of hell upon my own head. I try not to regret; but sometimes regret is important. Making amends; formulating a true and real apology; and living so that the world can see that you have made lasting changes—this is what healthy regret can look like. I made some terrible decisions, decisions that were worse than most. I paid for them; I had to pay. My dearest wish is that you will never have to pay for anything as badly as I did.

But let's leave regret to one side for a moment and concentrate on decision making.

The first thing I want to say is that we are trained to believe that there is a right or a wrong way to do things and that deciding which way to jump is as simple as pulling lever A or pushing button B. Should I have just gone on with my life quietly and not decided to tell my story and sell books out of the back of a car and have to be public about the murder? What would my life have been if I'd taken the "easier" road, the road that says, "Keep quiet, get a job, forget your past"? But my experience has taught me that life is not like that, not a simple equation of this or that. There's a poem by Robert Frost that you will no doubt be taught in school, because it feels as though every poetry class at some point studies this poem. You might know its most famous lines already:

> *Two roads diverged in a wood, and I—*
> *I took the one less traveled by,*
> *And that has made all the difference.*

I don't like this poem, and I don't like the fact that it's one of the few poems a lot of Americans know. I don't like it because it sets up an either/or proposition. In my mind, decision making looks nothing like two roads in a wood; I think it's more like the spokes of a bicycle wheel: they point each and every way, at every degree and angle, and knowing which way to go is hard.

It's even harder when the wheel is spinning. Think about when you ride your bike down the sidewalk: if you get enough speed up, the spokes all blur into one, right? That's what it can feel like to make a decision; there are so many options, and sometimes it's hard enough to tease out the separate strands that go into a decision, let alone make the right choice.

But let's slow down that wheel and stop awhile, here in the California sun, and consider each individual spoke. Each time you're faced with a decision, think of the bicycle wheel; work hard to separate the spokes, the strands of a decision, so that you can think clearly about which one you want to choose. That must always be your thought process: How do I choose the right and the good?

But there is something else you need to know, my boy. For young Black men, there are unseen spokes that the white culture holds in reserve for you. I don't mean white people; you will meet many good and true white people, just as you will meet Black people who don't have your best interests at heart. But the culture, the culture into which I and your mother have given you breath, has a whole set of spokes that you won't always be able to see: discrimination, a lack of opportunities, a sense that you can never measure up, all of it propagated by the school system, by grandparents who internalized white superiority and Black inferiority and handed them down to each subsequent generation, by media that know that fear of Black men in particular sells newspapers— that you must always hit a thousand when everyone else can get by hitting .300.

When I was in prison, your mother and I wrote often about the system that has created the food deserts in our communities, the War on Drugs that has filled our prisons, and the educational system that has proven itself ineffective when it comes to improving the lot of Black kids. One day I found myself writing this to your mother: "If given the opportunity they would still hang us from trees like 'Strange Fruit.' They have never stopped lynching us; they have only refined the way in which it is done."

I am sorry that I have to tell you about this, but it will inform your decisions even if you don't want it to. We have been lynched; we have been beaten; our leaders have been killed; we have been incarcerated and spat on and kept from the lunch counter. We have simply wanted to eat as our brothers and sisters have eaten, and yet . . . this is the great curse of our place in white culture. I want you to grow up free from the chains that have held so many of us back, but you can free yourself only if you know. And one thing to know is that there are spokes in the wheel that you can't even see.

I faced one such decision a few years ago, and in fact you made me make it. I was working for the Anti-Recidivism Coalition, a nonprofit that helps women and men reenter society after incarceration—in fact, I was its executive director. We were doing prison tours, helping people transition back to society, spending hours with newly released people talking about their experiences. We helped people get jobs in construction and firefighting and Hollywood, and we raised a ton of money. But mostly we helped people unpack their trauma, including some staff members. That was the heaviest part of the work—and the most beautiful—but I often felt we could never do enough.

There was so much hope amid the hurt, so much love amid the trauma. But it took a toll on me. One night, when we were living in Koreatown, you looked at me and said that I didn't look happy.

I decided to leave that job there and then. I had no idea what I was going to do, but I knew that running an organization that constantly put me proximate to prison life was too painful for me; it brought the trauma of my past to my daily life in the present. And as much as I wanted to help those who were newly released, I knew that for my own sense of well-being I needed a break.

It was a tough decision, but the importance of choosing happiness over prestige made it easy. It had been the perfect job for me, but it also had the possibility of being disastrous.

I could never have made that decision without your love, Sekou; without your being present, aware, and deeply emotionally smart. When you told me I looked unhappy, you once again saved my life. I wonder how many times you'll do that before our time on this planet is over.

Dad

The Freedom to Cry

Dear Sekou and Jay,

Sekou, you were crying this morning, and it doesn't matter about what—your tears were wonderful. No, I don't want to see you sob, and yes, I feel terrible when you're upset. But our world needs your tears. They are as important as the rain that seldom falls here in Los Angeles. For so long, young Black men like you have been unable to cry, unwilling to show their sadness, disallowed from the deeper feelings. So whenever you cry, I feel both sad for you as your father and happy for the world.

Jay, there was one time you cried that stands out for me. During one of our visits, I remember you getting really cranky, as toddlers will. You didn't want to be consoled, but then you noticed a woman across the room, and you ran over to her, climbed up into her lap, and fell asleep. I wasn't allowed to go get you from that stranger; it was so painful in a sense, but I gained comfort from watching how the woman cradled you and wiped your tears away and rubbed your head until you fell asleep.

That was the joy and sadness of visits. Not being able to pick you up was all sadness, but seeing you receive comfort for your tears? All joy.

Sekou, you've seen me cry. The song "True Love" by Loaded Lux breaks me every time I hear it, and I've never hidden that from you. But this isn't usually how it goes. From an early age, we're taught that it's not okay to cry—in fact, about the only feeling we're allowed to show is anger. I learned that as early as anyone. One day I was learning to ride a bike without training wheels. I was speeding down Camden Street in Detroit, the street I grew up on, and the bike kept going faster and faster, causing me to run into a telephone pole face-first and scraping most of the skin off the left side of my face. I ran in crying to my mother, who merely asked, "What you crying for?," put some peroxide on the wound, and sent me back out to ride the bike once again.

When we do cry, it tends to be when someone inspirational or famous dies. Take January 26, 2020, for example, a foggy Sunday morning on the West Coast. The world was different then; the first Covid-19 infection in the United States had just been announced, but it was just one person, and we all went about our lives as though nothing was wrong. Wuhan, the city in China where the infection had started, had been on lockdown for just three days. By the end of 2020, more than 325,000 people in the United States had died of the illness, including my friend Marlowe Stoudamire, a brilliant Detroit-based entrepreneur and business developer.

But that was all to come. That morning in LA, everywhere was hushed. Heavy clouds had rolled in off of the Pacific until they hung like a pall over the whole area, from Orange County to Malibu. The fog was thick. Voices barely carried. I imagined you up early at home with your mother, ready to face another happy day.

I was starting to think about getting ready to attend the Grammys that evening. My stylist was about to arrive—imagine that, from being in prison to having my own stylist for the Grammys—when I got a text from your mother.

About thirty miles from our house, up in the Malibu Canyon, a helicopter with nine people on board had crashed at around 9:45 A.M. Some mountain bikers had seen the impact and called 911. At 11:25, TMZ reported that one of the passengers on the chopper had been basketball star Kobe Bryant. Also on board were his daughter Gianna and seven other people, all on their way to a basketball game that Kobe was supposed to coach. Kobe was forty-one, his daughter just thirteen. In an instant, their lives had been extinguished in the fog of a Sunday morning.

We heard the news and wept.

Kobe was extraordinary not just for his basketball skills but for everything else. On top of his five NBA titles, two Olympic gold medals, and eighteen All-Star Game appearances, he was a musician, an actor, a published author, a philanthropist, a businessman, a father, a husband. He stood for Black success and excellence.

Seven months later, another extraordinary Black man died in our city: Chadwick Boseman. Boseman once said that the Marvel movies he had starred in—with mostly Black casts and Black directors—had changed what it means to be "young, gifted, and Black." But he had struggled with colon cancer for four long years, all the time still working, still raising money and awareness and helping our community and our country. He lost his fight on August 28, 2020.

We heard the news and wept.

About a year before Kobe died, on another Sunday, the rapper and entrepreneur Nipsey Hussle was standing outside his store, Marathon Clothing, just ten minutes south of our house in South LA. It was his community; in addition to the clothing store, he owned a burger joint, a barbershop, and a fish market nearby. He employed people in the neighborhood who otherwise couldn't get jobs, and he once even gave shoes to every student at a local elementary school.

Nipsey Hussle was a beacon of hope and a living example to all of us. He stood shining at the epicenter of hip-hop's "get-it-how-you-live" ethos, a path to success laid down by Master P, P. Diddy, Jay-Z, 50 Cent, Nas, and many others before him. Those titans of hip-hop, like their predecessors, built their art out of poverty, desperation, and street hustling. The ethos said, "I will take the broken pieces of my circumstances and create something beautiful, powerful, and enduring." It launched a cultural revolution that survived the War on Drugs and mass incarceration and created a voice for the voiceless. That so much of what they did was dismissed as glorifying violence only proved that they were onto something true and real.

But that terrible Sunday, a man walked up to Nipsey's clothing store with a gun. Nipsey was hit ten times and died.

We heard the news and wept.

One of Nipsey's greatest posthumous gifts was that he restored to us that which we didn't know we were missing. Days after he died, I talked to many brothers in person and via social media who expressed deep sorrow and admitted to having broken down in tears when they heard the news. For many, it was the first time they publicly shared their deepest sorrows, sadness, and tears. In a culture that suffocates or just plain denies our right to be tender and vulnerable, the reaction of those men was wonderful to behold. Their tears cleansed, nurtured, and normalized vulnerability for boys who had been taught to suppress their emotions so they could survive.

Like Tupac's and Biggie's before him, Nipsey's death weighed heavy on us—and for good reason. Like many of us, Nipsey could see beyond the circumstances of the hood he'd grown up in, past the straitjacket of his past misdeeds. He refused to be locked in by ideas that limited his imagination; he refused to keep his dreams to himself. Instead, he concentrated on the idea of family, community, art, and future on *his* terms. He made bold moves and took calculated risks; he stayed when others might have run (once you're successful, there can be an undercurrent of danger to your success). The streets were a runway for him to soar and teach our children that they could transcend the clouds of their circumstances; it devastated us that those same streets would kill him. Nipsey's death has forced us to examine ourselves in ways we hadn't in a long time and to accept the complexities of our lives.

Nipsey wasn't perfect, but why do Black men—and Black artists especially—have to be perfect? They don't have to be, and neither do you two. His very existence is proof that you can be the things you say in songs—an incredible effort of turning a vision board into an action board. As just one of the many things he accomplished, remember that he organized a peace treaty in hoods across the nation, all so that our world is a little safer. From South Central LA to South Side Chicago, from Detroit to Oakland, the potential for giants to be awakened and enlightened is in place thanks to him.

When Nipsey died, we wept just as my father's generation had wept decades earlier, when we had lost Malcolm X, Martin Luther King, Jr., and Patrice Lumumba. But these are often the only times that Black men—young Black men especially—feel free to lay down their pain and weep. Only when our heroes are killed are we able to express our feelings. Black men's tears are allowed when the rest of the world is grieving with us. But the rest of the time, we're taught that we must suppress our feelings or else channel them into rage or inertia or comeuppance or revenge. We hear phrases like "Go out there and fight or get your ass beat at home" or "Stop crying unless I give you something to cry for" or "Stop acting like a little bitch." We don't cry at births or graduations or when someone is successful, when someone shows he or she needs compassion and love, or when we just need to relieve the pressure. We don't cry when someone in our family comes to us in need, when a friend's clothes are in rags, or when our children are hungry. We don't cry when a virus hits our community harder than any other. We don't cry for so many reasons.

Our heroes die, and it devastates us—but what about the other deaths, the daily, ordinary deaths in our communities?

Perhaps we cried for George Floyd and Breonna Taylor; perhaps our tears fell for Trayvon Martin or Rayshard Brooks or Philando Castile. But the victims in our own communities, do we cry for them? And if not, why not? Have we become numb? Maybe that's why each of these losses hits us so hard; they jar us out of our numbness. Think about Detroit. There were 275 homicides there in 2019 alone. By October 2020, there had been 261 homicides in Los Angeles this year. How can we be numb to these numbers?

I was at Carson City Correctional Facility when we heard that Tupac Shakur had died. The news of his death devastated the men at the prison. The sounds of "Dear Mama," "California Love," and "Ambitionz az a Ridah" could be heard drifting beneath the door of nearly every cell on the tier. The mood was somber, contemplative. Through whispered conversations we considered our own role in his murder—yes, *our* role. No, none of us had pulled the trigger; we all loved him, his music, his stance on social issues, his fire. Nevertheless, we felt like coconspirators because we had lived the kind of life that Tupac and many other rappers rap about in their songs. We had lived it, and he had written about it, but it worked the other way around, too—he had written about it, so some of us had lived it. Whatever the case, we felt responsible that morning in September 1996.

We loved him because he had been so emotional, so vulnerable when he started out. Songs like "Brenda's Got a Baby," about a teenage mother who had gotten pregnant as the result of having sex with her cousin, brought home to me the sadness of your abandonment, Jay (not to mention that your mother's name is Brenda). No one else was writing like that about social issues, about personal issues, about the things that we lived and felt; we knew he'd come about it honestly, too. His family background had been one of resistance. His mother, Afeni, had raised him to think he was "the Black Prince of the revolution," he said, and he'd been surrounded by activists and revolutionaries as a child. He knew what it meant to be Black in America: in a deposition he once said, "There are no Shakurs, black male Shakurs, out right now, free, breathing, without bullet holes in them or cuffs on his hands. None." That was a radical statement from a rapper. He hadn't been content to simply enjoy the spoils of his celebrity; he was forging a new identity, one that could take on the societal ills he saw. We felt that Tupac would be a leader, could make a difference. The song "Changes," for example, highlighted so much about the Black experience. We truly believed he'd create the changes he rapped about; if nothing else, he poured light into the darkness. He was our hope; we felt he could be someone who created real change in our communities.

But Tupac faced so many of the things so many of us faced—the injustices and prejudices—and those things shaped him. He was shot in a recording studio in New York City in November 1994, but a year earlier he had been accused of rape in a hotel room. Though he always denied involvement in the sexual assault, he was honest enough to admit that he hadn't done anything to safeguard the woman involved. He was convicted and sent to a high-security prison in upstate New York. From there, everything changed. Bailed out by Death Row Records, he came out of imprisonment with a sense of rage that was unlike the artist who'd gone into jail. How could he be the same after the degradation of incarceration? His videos now seemed less like social activism and more like resentment and anger. He became belligerent; there were fights and taunts. Less than a year later he was dead, killed in a drive-by shooting in Las Vegas. He had just turned twenty-five years old.

Six months later, when it was announced that the Notorious B.I.G. had been killed—shot in Los Angeles after a party—the response in the prison population was nearly identical. Biggie was one of our best storytellers and probably the funniest. He had swagger but wasn't above using self-deprecation to punctuate his art.

By then I had been relocated to Oaks Correctional Facility in western Michigan. From cell to cell you could hear "Hypnotize," "Somebody's Gotta Die," or "Juicy" playing on the small radios we kept. It was another devastating blow to the hip-hop community, a not-so-gentle reminder that those of us who came from the streets had a job to do when it came to ending gun violence. The deaths of two of hip-hop's biggest names signaled a bittersweet turning point for a culture that was grappling with an East Coast/West Coast beef and the question of whether artists should be free to rap about murder, drug selling, and mayhem.

And then, all those years later, I was walking to courtside seats about to watch the Golden State Warriors play basketball when I heard that Nipsey had been killed. Like him, I was now running my own marathon; somehow, I had survived.

Yet we lost him, too, and we sat down and wept.

★ ★ ★

Where do tears come from?

I didn't cry from 1988 through 2007. In fact, I hadn't cried since the night I had attempted suicide at the age of sixteen. Ever since then, I thought I'd lost the ability to cry.

Years into my prison sentence, I found myself in the visiting room of a prison in Newberry, Michigan. I was talking with a friend about my feelings as my parole board hearing loomed. It was a highly charged time for me; as the hearing came closer, the injustices I faced on a daily basis seemed focused like the sun through glass, setting fire to the grass all around me. I had been transferred from a prison where I'd refused to work two jobs; at the new facility, they had placed me in solitary for seven days without cause, leading to my security being increased for no reason.

That day, I was telling my friend about how much I wanted to be the best father I could be, and out of nowhere, tears started to fall from my eyes. Instead of the old feelings of shame and fear, I was filled with a new mixture of empowerment and freedom. Would this be seen as weakness or strength? I didn't know; all I knew was that I knew nothing about the place where those tears came from. I had been taught long and hard to avoid tears—especially in prison, where strength and the appearance of strength count for so much. But that day, I loved you, Jay, so much that I loved you enough to cry. Those tears were the perfect soil to plant the seeds of freedom. If I was going to make it on the outside, I needed to feel human before I got out of that place. And nothing made me feel more human than the thought of being your dad once my sentence was finally over.

Eventually, the visit was over, and I went back to my cell.

But a set of tectonic plates had shifted in me, somewhere out of sight. I realized that even there, back in that tiny box of pain, I was now freer. It's hard to express just how much of a change that was. For decades I had battened down my humanity, bound it like an enslaved person's wrists. As I dug into those new feelings, Jay, my tears of sorrow for you turned into tears of joy for the possibility of a fully lived future. I knew that I could now feel and emote without giving a damn what anyone else thought. The fact of my tears was a sign that I was growing new skin, a skin that would surround a human being.

Your grandfather cried when our family was breaking up. I've talked to men on the phone who have wept at a lost relationship, at frustration with trying to build a life for themselves. Those tears have been priceless for me. The public nature of tears creates a community, a place in which emotions pass back and forth. They are the root of how we stop feeling so isolated; to share our tears means we are willing to be vulnerable, and that vulnerability invites others into our hearts.

Together with the Detroit social entrepreneur Shawn Wilson, former Detroit mayor Dave Bing, and the rapper Big Sean, in 2015 I created a movement called Men of Courage. Backed by the Ford Fund, this is a grassroots organization for Black men, specifically centered around storytelling. No one tells a story better than Big Sean. And you know what else? No one cries better than he does, either! There's a wonderful video of him performing at the Palace of Auburn Hills. After about two minutes of singing "Memories," he sits on the edge of the stage and just weeps. His tears come from many places—a friend struggling with addiction; his struggles with suicidal ideation; the miscarriage of his child. His albums are highly emotional records, and I honor him for that. (He's cried with me on panels, too.)

Just listen to the reaction of the crowd when he breaks down on that video. There are no jeers; there are no boos; there's a kind of quiet as the crowd try to work out why he's no longer singing, and then when they realize he's crying, they cheer his show of emotion. He is loved even more for being a man who can show his vulnerabilities. We must honor a man like Big Sean, just as we must honor all boys and men who have the courage to cry. What a gift Big Sean's tears are to Black boys.

Sekou and Jay: you are free to cry as much as you need to. I wrote in *Writing My Wrongs* about my lack of tears after I was shot: "My pistol became my therapy. Instead of crying tears, I cried bullets that deeply impacted my community." This can never be your way, as I wish it had never been mine. But I did not have the advantages you now have; your emotions are honored. I want you both to be fully human, fully awake, fully in awe of how your tears can move our world forward, can release the pressure in yourself and your community, a kind of sustaining rain. Don't ever apologize for your tears, and don't just save them for the moments when the world loses a star, a hero, or someone else famous. Use your tears for good, to show that you are gentle and soft and emotionally open to grief and joy and whatever else brings those tears to your eyes.

Let your tears be what you are known for, not violence or anger or disenchantment. Only then can we start out on the true road of redemption.

Dad

Death Row Sons

Dear Jay,

Man, it was a blessing meeting you today. My pops said he knows all about your story, he said he has your book. He's on Death Row up North in San Quentin. Major Love and Respect

I was riding with a car service a few months ago and got to talking to the young driver, K Jr. He told me he was in college, engaged, and in love, with the whole world ahead of him. I took to him immediately; he was smart and thoughtful. We discussed his studies, his hopes for the future, his fiancée, even the books he was reading. Eventually I told him about *Writing My Wrongs.*

As I described my book, I noticed that K Jr. grew quiet. I figured he was just concentrating on the ride, or maybe it was one of those moments when a new acquaintanceship dries up like the seed that falls on rocky land in the Bible: "A farmer went out to sow his seed. . . . Some fell on rocky places, where it did not have much soil. It sprang up quickly, because the soil was shallow. But when the sun came up, the plants were scorched, and they withered because they had no root." Some relationships aren't meant to grow.

Still, when we arrived at my destination, we exchanged numbers, and something about that young man stayed with me as I went about my day.

That same evening, my phone buzzed—it was a text from K Jr. telling me that his father was on death row in San Quentin.

That text broke my heart. Here was a young man, so full of hope, love, and optimism, living with the reality that his father was waiting to be killed. I thought about K Jr.'s future graduation, his upcoming marriage, and all the other things he'd have to do while shouldering the weight of his father's death sentence. I thought about his courage, fortitude, and will to make a life for himself, while the man who had given him life fought endlessly to stop the state from taking his own. I had known that day that our meeting had been a divine calling; that it was meant, not accidental.

Months later, I was hurtling north over the Golden Gate Bridge to an event at San Quentin. It was a gentle, beautiful day in San Francisco. I'd left early, watching as a breeze ran across the bay, lifting rows of whitecaps into the morning sun. As I turned onto I-580 to join the traffic speeding over the Richmond Bridge, I watched all the cars and wondered how many of the people in them knew that below them on the headland, the oldest prison in California held more than three and a half thousand men. San Quentin's death row is the largest in the United States. More than seven hundred of the men in that prison—737 by early 2019, according to the *Los Angeles Times*—are housed in the euphemistically named "Condemned Unit."

There are just fifty-six countries on the planet that carry out the death penalty; many others have death penalty statutes but no longer execute their citizens. As I passed through the creaky wrought-iron security gates of the facility, I marveled at that fact: that we in this country are barbarians; that to us, housing people in cages until we execute them is considered a perfectly acceptable form of justice. Since March 2019, there has been a moratorium on carrying out death sentences in the state of California, yet the men remain there, cooped up in small cages, condemned by their fellow citizens to rot forever, hopeless, forgotten, damned.

San Quentin opened in July 1852, just two years after California became a state. The state's gold rush was winding down, *Uncle Tom's Cabin* had recently been published, and Frederick Douglass was giving his "The Hypocrisy of American Slavery" speech in which he said:

> I say it with a sad sense of disparity between us. I am not included within the pale of this glorious anniversary! Your high independence only reveals the immeasurable distance between us. The blessings in which you this day rejoice are not enjoyed in common. The rich inheritance of justice, liberty, prosperity, and independence bequeathed by your fathers is shared by you, not by me. The sunlight that brought life and healing to you has brought stripes and death to me.

But here, sixty-eight inmates were being transferred from a prison ship in San Francisco Bay to the new building. San Quentin is the oldest prison in California that wasn't a ship, a sprawling complex of old buildings, perched precariously on land that oversees a magical view of the bay. I imagine real estate developers would die for a piece of that land. The water looks serene from a distance at least, and on a clear day like this, you can look across the bay and see the monied skyline of San Francisco, one of the most expensive places to live in America. But here the prison stands cold and indifferent—a blaze of hell on the beautiful edge of the roiling water.

These contradictions and others have shaped the narrative of this historic place. San Quentin is where George Jackson formed revolutionary ideas in the late 1960s and where he was shot and killed by a corrections officer on August 21, 1971, in the yard outside the Adjustment Center. It's where the Nobel Peace Prize nominee and alleged gang leader Stanley Tookie Williams III appealed his conviction for twenty-six years. Despite an international groundswell of support and protests against his being put to death, he lost all appeals and was executed on December 13, 2005. If you look at the *Los Angeles Times* website and its list of the 737 men who were on death row at the start of 2019, you'll see a sea of faces of color. Sure, there are white faces, but mostly it's Black and Latino men staring back at you. By early 2020, the numbers were 259 Black, 189 Latino, and 239 white. If you add in other races (Native American and Asian), 77 percent of men on death row in San Quentin are people of color.

One of those faces belongs to Kevin Cooper. Cooper escaped from prison in 1983 and holed up in a house in Chino

Hills. As he hid, a quadruple homicide took place in a nearby house, for which Cooper was convicted and sent to death row. He has consistently denied involvement, and there is plenty of evidence of police and prosecutorial malfeasance in the case. Cooper is currently fighting to have his innocence proven through DNA testing. Like the hundreds of other men slated for execution inside the egg yolk yellow building, Cooper is embroiled in the fight of his life. It's a brutal and unforgiving process; decades pass while men's lives are stalled, the blue skies outside their cells darkened by hopelessness.

Yet despite the gruesome nature of this environment, where hundreds of men have been convicted of killing and hundreds more wait to be killed, San Quentin is staking a claim as a model for reform. It's the kind of reform that keeps me hopeful that we will do more and afraid that we will think we have done enough. It was in this spirit that I joined nearly three hundred women and men volunteers that day to celebrate the opening of San Quentin's tech center.

The tech center, known as Code 7370, is stocked with all the modern equipment one would expect in a Silicon Valley facility, and its volunteers teach the men inside how to write computer code. The idea is to give them valuable tools that they will hopefully be able to use in the job market when they are released. It's the kind of effort that's crucial, given the surge in incarcerations. (Fully 25 percent of the world's incarcerated people are locked up in the United States, and the number has swelled by 700 percent since the time of George Jackson.) But plenty of people, both here and elsewhere, are not giving up.

This center of digital hope was born out of a partnership

between an innovative nonprofit called the Last Mile, the California Prison Industry, and the California Department of Corrections and Rehabilitation. This kind of cooperation was virtually unheard of decades ago, when people were just beginning to go online. Today there are more partnerships like this, which link the states, nonprofits, and corporate America.

I had arrived the night before and joined my friends and colleagues the next morning for pastries and coffee at a shop a mile or so from the prison. Imagine the scene: we checked and double-checked, to make sure we had our IDs and weren't wearing clothing that would violate prison rules. For some of the others, it was a new experience; for me, it was something else.

The familiarity of crashing iron as the gates slammed shut, coupled with the smell of processed food slopped onto plastic food trays, jarred me back to the memories of the nineteen years I had spent in prison. Something deep in me stirred; I felt that familiar sense of helplessness and heightened awareness that came from having to fend for myself in environments like this. The flavors, the smells, the sounds, the very air were known to me. I floated into and out of thoughts of the past until I was interrupted by the sound of a short, walnut brown, elderly Black man calling to me. He asked if I'd written the book that was circulating around the cell blocks, and when I told him I had, I watched his smile broaden. His smile felt right in my spirit—it was as a sacred gift and reminded me why I had come there, come back to prison. I shook his hand, and we embraced. As we did, I felt his thin, worn bones.

We headed to the chapel for a meeting, and within seconds

of stepping inside, I found myself hugging and greeting dozens of men of all races, all dressed in blue state-issued uniforms that showed the common inhumanity of incarceration. This blue is the great leveler, each uniform saying "I am here," a place where no one ever wants to be. I recognized some of the men from previous visits; some I was meeting for the first time. Each told me in his own way that he was proud of me, that my new life outside gave him hope. Their words urged my soul like the winds urged the water out there in the bay, a churn of conflicted feelings. I loved their hugs, their handshakes. I loved their voices, their various accents rising up into the roof of the chapel, a cavalcade of humanity still urgently trying to be positive, to give love. I was glad my book had reached those men; I was sad that it had had to do so.

I had promised my friends and mentors that I would serve when I got out of prison, that I would create something positive, that I would share the kindness they had given me—and here, on that day, I was repaying my promise in a tiny way. There was a sense of optimism amid the blue uniforms in that chapel. It felt like a high school reunion of sorts, except this wasn't high school, and not all of us would be leaving that day.

Eventually the crowd settled into their seats, and the program got under way. The dynamic duo of Beverly Parenti and Chris Redlitz, the founders of the Last Mile, were charming hosts and great emcees. MC Hammer, a longtime supporter and champion of the men, was in attendance, offering words of encouragement and empowerment. Graduates of the program—those who were now free and gainfully employed—shared their stories of success.

Later, my friend Scott Budnick, the founder of the

Anti-Recidivism Coalition (ARC), invited me and a group of other visitors to join him in a guided tour of the prison. Crossing the yard, we greeted many of the hundreds of men playing basketball, exercising, or playing chess. At one point, a young Black guy called to me, "Yo, what size are those shoes?" I told him and asked him if he was sizing me up; it was nice to be able to get a laugh out of him in all that darkness.

Then my heart sank; Scott invited me to join him in a visit to death row. A sour feeling gurgled up in my stomach. It didn't feel right to be going there, that bleak place where life can end at any moment, the block where men, brothers, uncles, friends, and fathers all wait to be put to death. What kind of world is it that can even conceive of such a place?

When we reached the unit, we were met by a tall white officer with a bright, cheery smile. Initially I found his smile unsettling—it seemed perverse, disrespectful. What was there to smile about? How could he be happy knowing these men were going to die on his watch? Was he just another sick racist fuck, the like of whom I knew all too well from my time in prison?

But these turned out to be snap judgments, informed by trauma. I was ignorant about that officer. In fact, I didn't know him from a can of paint; I had judged him based on my own experience of being in prison, and even though that smile meant he fit the description, it was not a correct assessment. When I spoke, he looked me in the eye and asked how he could help me. The truth was, he was a courteous man, thoughtful and professional amid all that death.

That place . . . Tiers went all the way up, five stories. Iron bars; dark; dreary. To the right of the officer there was an opening that led outside to the yard, where at least a hundred men were held in cages. Each cage held about twenty men. They looked like dog kennels, all in a row, men locked up like nothing more than animals in a city pound, corralled with ropes and sticks by an unfeeling world, left here in cages until their appeals finally ran out, their numbers were called, a last meal was proffered, they made the walk to death, from the cage to the chair. They were waiting to be euthanized, those poor men in cages—I wanted to scream the word "cages"—with no home save this barbaric place; they were no longer seen as human by the society that had failed them.

In that moment, I thought of what Malcolm X had written in his autobiography:

> Any person who claims to have deep feeling for other human beings should think a long, long time before he votes to have other men kept behind bars—caged. I am not saying there shouldn't be prisons, but there shouldn't be bars. Behind bars, a man never reforms. He will never forget. He never will get completely over the memory of the bars.

I wanted to scream "What the hell is wrong with this world? Why do people think dehumanizing and degrading people is the solution?"

But it was not the moment to scream; it was the moment to connect, or at least try to. So I went to where the men on death row were held in cages. I tried saying hello to some of them, to make some kind of connection with them. But all I could actually mumble was "Hey." What do you say to men who are waiting to be put to death by the state? I felt inadequate. This was horror.

Eventually, a middle-aged Black man called out to me, "Hey, are you Shaka, the guy who wrote that book?" His eyes lit up when I greeted him. "A brother named K let me read your book, he said you knew his son. Hey, man, I write too. This is my book." It all came in a rush of words as he shoved a piece of paper through the gate into my hand with his book cover on it. That man—defeated by the system, in thrall to his own death, yet hopeful still—had written a book, an act of ultimate hope in the future. But as I stuffed the paper into my pocket, anything he said after that sounded as though he was underwater, because the only thing reverberating in my mind was the sound of K's name.

The man I'd heard about during that serendipitous ride . . . here he was, in this awful place, less than a hundred feet from where I stood. I knew then that I had to speak to him, I needed to see his face, see his eyes, and hear his voice. I had to see him.

I went into the cell block and told an officer about my exchange with the man in the cage outside, the one who had written an entire book. I asked him if I could go up to the fourth tier where K was locked in his cell, but it was denied me. I wanted to tell them then that I had been in cell blocks for nearly two decades, that I knew it was possible, that I knew what it meant to be in a cage, knew what it meant to wait, wait, wait—but I refrained. Fortunately, the lieutenant sent an officer up to K's cell to ask if he wanted to come down and meet me. I stood at the officer's desk for what felt like an eternity, waiting for an answer. Finally, the officer returned and said that K had agreed to come down.

Time seemed to stop. Seconds stretched to minutes stretched to what felt like hours. But then K appeared with his hands cuffed behind his back. When he saw me, his eyes lit up and a smile slowly creased his face. He looked young and vibrant, somehow, even though he was caged like all the other men.

He was placed in a cell inside a small room; I found myself standing on the outskirts, looking at him through the bars. "It's good to see you," we said simultaneously. The coincidence of our shared words caused us to smile and shook free all my words and feelings about his son, K Jr.

K beamed with pride as I told him about our various text messages and how thoughtful I had found his son to be. I talked about his love for his fiancée and how focused he was on school; they were all things K already knew, but I hoped my voice recounting those things might underline for him just how special K Jr. had become. I felt like an uncle bragging on my nephew to the man who had raised him.

K told me about the things he had shared with his son over the years: the importance of getting an education, of working hard, all the usual things, but they felt different coming from K, from that place. Tears welled up in my eyes, because despite his circumstances, K had found a way to reach his son's heart. He had found a way to bestow lessons on his son that had urged him onto a path to graduating from college, not onto a path that led to prison or death row. K had not given up on or given in to his circumstances. He had fostered dignity in his son, had found a way to be a father, a mentor, and above all a man. Somehow, he'd done those things from a cell on tier four in the death row cell block inside San Quentin.

K is a reflection of what I believe about fatherhood. Like transformation, fatherhood can happen anywhere when we create the space for it to blossom. Jay, I failed in my attempts to foster these things while I was in prison. Even after prison, we have had our share of difficulties in creating the kind of bond that K and K Jr. have created. But if those two men can become as one; if Mandela could survive to lead his country; if Malcolm X could change the world; if our brothers and sisters have triumphed over and through the walls all around us, then we, too, can figure this out.

This is the hope that I held out there that day as that man's book lay crumpled in my pocket, as K wished me well and I turned to leave, as the bay and the city sparkled in the afternoon air, as the car that had brought me there turned out of the gates of San Quentin and headed out toward who knows where.

Dad

The Ford Taurus

Dear Sekou and Jay,

By 2016, if someone had been looking at me from the outside, things must have seemed pretty rosy. I had the book deal I had yearned for; people were starting to say nice things about me and recognize the new man I had become; the media were calling for interviews—one day it was Oprah Winfrey, the next, Trevor Noah, and on and on. Money was coming in, good money, and I suppose I looked "successful," whatever that means. I had been five years out of prison, and each day put that horror one step farther behind me.

But the truth was, on the inside, I felt miserable. Why did I think that my time inside would ever fully recede? It was part of me now, that much I knew. I was struggling to make a success of my writing and speaking careers. My relationship wasn't working. I was building up my finances but still struggling. Beyond the writing I was working two and a half jobs, teaching, keeping up a fellowship. Every day was a battle, and often I felt I was losing that fight. Some mornings, just getting out of bed took effort, like trying to pull a great weight up a hill. I regularly stood at the bottom of that hill and looked up, unable to move.

It was during that time that I decided to leave Detroit and move to California.

I thought a change of scenery would restore optimism to my heart and give me a shot of hope—and what a change, from freezing winters to year-round 70 degrees and sunny skies. I had traded on optimism so far, and it had helped here and there. I figured that in a looser place, one of palm trees and sea breezes and the vibrancy of a city built on Hollywood's glamour, hope could take root inside me and get me to a better place.

It didn't take me long to realize that the environment hadn't been the problem; what happens inside a person is far more important than what's going on outside.

There were truly dark times.

Shortly after my book was published, I went on tour to publicize it, and for several weeks I told and retold the story of my worst moments to readers, to journalists, to audiences, to people I met along the way. That was the nature of the endeavor, of course; like many authors, my job was to drum up interest in my story, and one of the most effective ways is to show up, talk, listen to questions, answer them, open up, always open up, tell stories, tell stories, tell stories. The words I repeated, the terrible things to which I confessed over and over—sometimes they could feel like just words. But mostly, I was repeatedly dragged back into my worst experiences, reopening and revisiting profound traumas with no idea how to process them away from the glare of faces turned my way. It was no one's fault, not even my own, but to continually recount the worst parts of my life, to every day take a knife to my skin without numbing myself beforehand . . . the blood flowed, and I could not stop it. All that pain just pooled inside me, behind my eyes, deep in an untouchable part of me.

Once the microphones went quiet, once the lights were turned off, once the hotel room door latched and another night on the road found me in a small room in a distant city, my luggage, sitting there next to my bed every time I opened my eyes, was the past and everything that had happened and what I'd paid for it and the feelings I had for that younger self and the feelings I had for me here, now, away from family and friends, another night of retelling it all looming ahead in my mind, keeping me from sleep.

I told myself it was for the greater good—for the connected sakes of atonement, redemption, and advocacy. The sea of incarcerated faces kept me out there, on the road, telling their stories through my own, telling my story so that they might one day feel the release of forgiveness and freedom. That was what I told myself; but the reality is that there is no greater good than taking care of and nurturing your own self, giving succor to your own heart, giving your own mind a place to rest. I had no desire to be an emotional martyr, but I felt, too, that it was my job to tell the truth about the pain and devastation my actions had caused to my family and to the family of the man I'd killed. So what if the hotel rooms were empty and cold? So what if the luggage of my past loomed like dark shapes behind blackout shades? So what if the nights of torment were like the distant sound of the freeways beside which motels unrestfully lie?

My purpose overrode these high ideals: I had to help other young men avoid the same pitfalls that had claimed my youth. If I lay awake in torment, hadn't something in my past prepared me for that? More damagingly, I've wondered since then if my guilt over the past made me think I had it coming, that desperation of the road. In short, I asked myself, who was I to complain?

For five years straight I had ripped open the wounds of my past for the world to see.

Was it any wonder that in the midst of that effort, I lost my sense of self-love? I acted as though I was having the time of my life. I used phrases like "I am grinding" or "I am hyperfocused," and I used them so much and for so long I think I came to believe that they described something true and something real. (Spoiler alert: those words were empty.) If I was so busy getting shit done, how could there be time to feel? This empty hotel room—does it contain that time? How about this car ride to the airport or this flight—is there time here to feel? All this grinding and hyperfocus—does it have to be so encompassing that every second of every day is about purpose? What about the purpose of my own survival?

The reality is that there was plenty of time in those hotel rooms, on those car rides, in those airplanes, in those moments when to feel would have been a joy. But I repeatedly denied myself that option. *Don't you see I've got fucking souls to save?*

★   ★   ★

I don't suppose you'll be surprised to hear that I thought sex might help me fill the void. Even less surprised, I imagine, to hear that it only made what was empty even more bottom-lessly dark. Matthew 13: "For whoever has, to him more will be given, and he will have abundance; but whoever does not have, even what he has will be taken away from him." I broke hearts easily with no thought of the other person's life beyond my conquest. Love felt like a bullshit emotion; I couldn't capture it, contain it, or maintain it. Most of the time, I couldn't even feel it. Was that what I had survived prison for? To have sex that led nowhere; to drink too much; to buy shit I didn't need? Had I survived only to awake alone again in a hotel room, no note on the cold pillow next to me, the minibar empty, the latest sneakers thrown into the corner?

What hurt most was that there were only certain parts of me that people could love—my sense of humor, my thought-fulness, my resourcefulness—or so I thought. This is what incarcerating a child does: it erects an instant and unbreak-able barrier between the boy in prison and the man who years later is "free" and wants to love and be loved. All I wanted, deep deep deep down, was that love, a love rooted in under-standing that would allow me to just be. That would make me feel nurtured and taken care of. That would make me feel fully seen. I wanted to be able to express anger and disappointment without their being attached to my nineteen-year-old self.

But I knew that however many times I told my story in public, there would always be a depth to it that no other per-son could understand. Shit, I wouldn't *want* another person to understand it; I wouldn't wish my experiences upon anyone.

It was hard for me to trust anyone. In my dating life, I felt as though women were attracted to the idea of me rather than the real me. But in each new relationship, I faced from the very first second not just the threat of that barrier—not just of what cannot be empathized with or understood—but another, more insidious barrier: the things I spoke of, the violence and death and depravity of prison; those were things that I could never love about myself, either. It was not as simple as being on a date and telling a potential new partner about a job that was horrible or the death of a family member or whatever setbacks normal people chat about. It was something else entirely. It was trying to find the words to tell someone that I had committed murder without fear of her recoiling in horror. That the sound of fireworks unnerves me (is that gunfire aimed at me?). Sometimes, to this day, I wake up in the middle of the night drenched in sweat as my body expels the experiences I went through in solitary. Think of the things you can't love about yourself, and then imagine revealing them to other people every night for weeks.

Then imagine this: a beautiful new friend, who may or may not one day be a romantic partner, wanting to get to know me better, and me her, suggested the most innocent and intimate and positive thing anyone could want to do with another human being. She said, "Let's go on a walk."

And this was what I could *not* say to her, as I turned down her kind offer: "I got fucking shot when I was walking."

No, I had never processed that moment. Each day was an effort to learn to walk again.

★   ★   ★

I could learn to walk again—I had to do so. But would the world let me?

As a child I lived the life of an outlaw. I was doing bad shit, and though I tried not to get caught, at least there would be a natural logic to it if I did. I still had a sense of right and wrong, of action followed by consequence. That meant that I could still retain a certain grim optimism: there was still an expectation that if I toed the line, the right things would happen. That feeling never left me (and probably made prison even harder than it might otherwise have been; I wasn't so far gone that I couldn't still see, taste, smell, sense injustice).

After prison, the sense remained: I'd paid for my mistakes, and if I did the right things—toed the line, kept out of trouble, kept my driver's license and car registration up to date, got a job, and made money—the world would leave me alone and good things would accrue.

But then moments like this kept happening: One night I was at a friend's bar in a suburb of Detroit called Livonia. I found myself talking to a woman—a new, casual friend, nothing serious. Eventually I felt like stepping outside to smoke a cigar. It had been a hot day in Detroit, and my friend was in sandals, but by the evening the cooling winds were blowing off Lake St. Clair, so we sat in my car—a nice new Taurus, if you must know, replete with all the bells and whistles—so at least she could keep warm while I smoked.

Just like that, a young white police officer shows up and taps on the window. "Hey, what are you doing?" he asks.

"I'm just smoking a cigar in my car," I say, "because it's a bit nippy out there."

"Do you have your license?"

Now, I'm not even moving at this point—I'm not driving anywhere. There's no probable cause here. But I can see something in the officer's eyes—how did he *get* this car, this nice car, in this neighborhood?—all the usual things. Here's the deal, though: I am fucking *loving* this because I have a damned license, and I have insurance and current registration and I like my car, and it's all good. "And no, Officer," I say as I hand him my license, "I don't have anything illegal on me."

After a bit he comes back to the car, he gives back my ID, my registration, and says, "Everything came back good."

And as he's saying this, I glance into the rearview mirror and there are five police cruisers sitting there.

The camera of my story pans at this point to the young lady in the car with me. What must she think? Who is she sitting with in this vehicle? I know her only casually, and though I haven't done shit, she can't know that.

Sure enough, I'm invited to step out of the vehicle. The car has an automatic starter, so I keep the keys in my pocket. As I get out, my jacket is swinging and I stop it with my hand, and the cop asks me, "What's that?"

"It's my car key," I say, but before I can show him, he grabs my hand and puts it behind my back.

"You're not under arrest," he says, "but for my safety, you know?"

I say, "*Your* safety? What about *my* safety? You're the one with the gun."

Okay, Shaka, maintain control—don't let this slip into some shit that's unnecessary. But I am a man, you know? I'm forty-some years old, many of those years spent in the

American prison system. Why am I in a parking lot with five or six police surrounding me and I haven't done shit? It's embarrassing. This new friend doesn't really know me, and now some flatfoot has my arm behind my back.

Just as I'm calming myself, a sergeant steps up and says, "So. Tell me about the murder in 1991."

I have told the world about the murder. I have told the world about the life I led that brought me to that terrible point. I have told the world about the forgiveness for which I begged and that I was fortunate to receive. I have told the world about my hopes for other incarcerated children and men and women, my dreams of a new way of looking at how we rehabilitate instead of punishing. I have told the world about the debasement of prison life. I have told folks, as I told that sergeant that night in Livonia, that I am a teacher (then at the university of Michigan) and an advocate, and a man trying to give and receive love—but I have never told the world, nor you, my dear sons, about the nights when the luggage looms in the darkness. The nights when I am forced to breathe, really breathe, take a step away from yet another ledge, and remake myself once again before the dawn arrives.

I spent many years in prison, but Sergeant, I am no longer incarcerated or even on parole, truths you ignore when you refer to my conviction in 1991 as though I am a murderer rather than someone who, as a child, committed murder. I understand that as a quasi–military force you need a bad guy, and what you found on your cruiser's little computer was my name and the date 1991 and a conviction. I realize that your attitude changed when you realized I teach at the fucking

University of Michigan and am a fellow at the MIT Media Lab, and I write books—and yes, feel free to buy one, there are some in the trunk of this Taurus.

I've served my time, Officer, though time will never let me alone. Given that, I should like now, Sergeant, while there's time, to be allowed to finish my cigar in my damned fine car and continue getting to know this damn fine woman, if you would be so kind.

What I learned eventually, once the luggage had been stowed away in my attic, was that I had everything I needed inside me to turn things around but I would have to take the first step toward reclaiming the best parts of me. The best parts were my sense of humor, my curiosity, my willingness to work hard, my service to the community—I was proud of those things. The stuff that no longer served was the partying, the sense of drifting, the relationships that were going nowhere. It all started with getting through the pain of each horrible moment, breathing into the pain and out again, because if you can get through the momentary suffering, you can come out on the other side stronger. I know this intimately. I spent two decades learning this, and that's what I did, boys; that's what I did.

Dad

Addiction

Dear Jay and Sekou,

It wasn't a good day to start with.

It began with the end of one of the most important relationships of my life: finally, Ebony and I were done. The breakup had been coming, but it never feels real until it actually happens; like a death, I suppose. We'd been through so much together, from our first correspondence to Sekou's birth and beyond; but now we knew that the forces pressing on us both, from all sides, were too heavy to navigate. And so into the stew of things choking me—the guilt, the pain, the PTSD, my attempts to work out who on earth I was—now I added this failure. Though we weren't actually married, our relationship mirrored that of a marriage, and when men are married, they live longer—you can look up the stats yourself. With Ebony, I had responsibilities— to be somewhere when I said I would, to do the things I'd promised to do. That was now gone. The only thing left was me, just as it had been for the last two decades.

I called one of my sisters and asked if she'd hang out. I'd missed her birthday by a week and wanted to make it up to her. Remembering that she loved lamb chops, I suggested a place I knew made the best damn chops in Detroit, a strip club. Yes, I went for lunch with my sister to a strip club during its day shift. A few more calls were made, and all my damn sisters showed up, and the party was on. We were doing shots, drinking champagne, the works—I was tipping and chatting, tipping and chatting, in my element, an image of freedom, I guess, though inside I was hurting hard from the events of the day. This, too, is sometimes how our community deals—alcohol isn't really seen as an addictive force, so when pain arrives, we bury it in drinking and partying, because what else are we going to do? At the time, I didn't know how to access a therapist, nor did I understand the relief that self-care could provide. Those things weren't generally talked about in my community and definitely not talked about in cell blocks, so why not live it up in a strip club with your sisters, one shot of Don Julio at a time?

Eventually, your uncle Smiley invited us to a different club where he was hosting a bunch of rappers—anything to keep the party going. I headed out to a bar to pick up my friend Jerry, and he drove us to the second club, where it was really on. Suddenly it was three in the morning, Jerry had disappeared, and I was left with that unhealthy mixture of alcohol and delusion: *Sure, I'm a better driver when drunk*. I jumped into my truck and headed for home.

Let me pause here and take you up above the scene; let's

watch it like we're a news helicopter. A man two years free from parole, a convicted felon, filled with liquor and pain, on a rainy Detroit night, drives away from a club. His truck . . . there it is, swishing along sleety streets, isolated and weaving, a little too fast, a little too sure. We don't know what he's doing or where he's going, but we'll follow him for as long as it takes. Rain and ice begin to pour down. There are no cops around, and we're hearing that he's done this enough nights that he's sure he'll make it home. It's a chain of terrible thinking, but like the drunken, howling man behind the wheel, let's not worry about that now. He is not in his neighborhood; he can barely see through the terrible weather. There, a freeway sign!

Now, listen, viewers, we're not sure where he's going. That's not an entrance to the freeway . . . No no no! That's the exit. We in the helicopter are screaming at him now, stop stop stop, that's the exit ramp! and he's heading down it, lost, angry and hurt, a free man and a man just off parole, a lost soul drunk, single, his child asleep somewhere, his sisters sleeping it off, and there he heads, down down down the exit ramp . . .

There's a curve, and a car swerves past him. Maybe this awakens in him the realization that he's in terrible danger. He might kill himself; he might kill someone else; he might just survive long enough to be pulled over, arrested, taken back to prison, see? Isn't that what those guards said? *See you soon, son! You'll be back! Your type is always back.*

By now, viewers, it's pretty clear that he understands the mistake he's made—he knows it's the exit ramp, but what can he do? Another car is coming around the exit curve, and he's pulling onto the embankment! And there he goes into oncoming traffic, his only hope, and he's turning around as fast as he can, still drunk, still sure he can make it home. And he's finally back on the exit ramp going the correct way . . . There he goes, safe at last, his knuckles white on the wheel. And now the weather forecast, brought to you by Heineken— drink responsibly . . .

It wasn't the first time I'd danced with disaster. A couple of years earlier, my parole agent thought I'd smoked some weed. What had actually happened was that I'd hung out at your aunt Vanessa's house, and your uncle Smiley was a big fan of the stuff, so by the time I'd left my clothes—hell, my eyebrows, probably—reeked of weed. I'd headed off to my parole meeting, and as usual I'd smoked a cigar in the car. But at the parole office, the officers shot me looks of suspicion, as though I would've risked everything for a toke (I didn't even smoke weed back then).

"We're going to do an instant drop," the parole officer said. He was irate. I knew the test would come back negative, but the specter of everything falling apart spooked me.

Imagine the shame I would have felt. Since I'd gotten out of prison, I'd created a career for myself; I was deep into fatherhood with Sekou; and I was free, finally, of the walls and the shit food and the violence and the sense of falling, always falling through the air, with no one to catch me. But when I got home that rainy night after my wrong-way drive, I was shaking, knowing that all the new and wonderful things would have gone away had red and blue lights flashed in my rearview. It brought to mind the degradation of being strip-searched, the mug shot, the clanking doors . . . having to leave a child behind once again.

Imagine the shame of that.

Back when I'd been nineteen, I'd faced those degradations as a child—all of them new. But I was a child no longer that night in Detroit. I was a man, and not just any man but a leader in my community, a voice in the fight against criminal injustice. I pictured the flick of a police light; me on the side of a rainy freeway, soaked; two officers running my details, not knowing what they'd find until they found it. And this, this disaster, this downfall, would serve only to underline everything the system thinks about someone like me: that we are incapable of righting our wrongs. What would I say to my father? To Sekou? To Ebony? To Jay? To the people who've supported me? To my colleagues at MIT? To the students I teach, the young people I mentor? All those folks who have championed me, now looking down from the helicopter, too, watching me fill like a water barrel with shame—the shame of consequences.

And with that came this image: a scratchy metal mirror in a prison cell, where I can hardly see my features, hardly make out the tone of my eyes, the stretch of the skin around my mouth, the different tones, the lines, the marks, the curve of my face, yet I can see one thing so clearly in that metal mirror: failure.

By the grace of God or the serendipity of the universe, I did not have to face those things. But I knew then that things must change. I could not put myself in that position ever again.

There was too much to lose.

★ ★ ★

This is how it all started.

I believe addiction is a by-product of shame and suppressed emotions and unhealed hurts. And I had the unfortunate chance to learn about all those things.

At fourteen years old, a life of pain was already my lot. I had been introduced to Detroit's drug culture by an older hustler; he had cash and power, two intoxicating things to a kid who had neither. It was the start of a terrible nourishment. I thought the guy would give me shelter from my dysfunctional, violent childhood, but as I told an interviewer years later, "Unfortunately the world just doesn't work like that. And like many vulnerable children, I got seduced into the drug trade by older, more seasoned street hustlers, and that's how it happens for a lot of kids."

It had been bad enough when heroin and cocaine had punctuated my city, but by late 1983, early 1984, the first crack houses were appearing. In a documentary series called *American Dope*, a Detroit hustler named BJ Chambers described what happened when he was part of creating the first wave of the crack epidemic. Originally, he had been selling weed, but in early 1984 he'd loaned a friend some money to sell a new, shiny drug called crack cocaine at a house on the corner of Newport and Jefferson, just about a mile from my childhood home. He'd given his friend twenty-four hours to make it work; by the time Chambers showed up at the house the next day, the friend had made $30,000, and a whole new hell had arrived.

Those were death packets, sold for cheap thrills to those who could least afford to pay, and the drug wasn't just for adults. I saw teenagers lured by the white toxic devil smoke, scorching their growing lungs, the euphoric intoxication promised them the good life in a city that had once been thriving. According to a Black former undercover DEA agent, John Sutton, there "was something missing [in Detroit] . . . there was a tremendous erosion of the political system, an erosion of the police department, an erosion of the religious system in this city." Just as Sutton didn't say that with any sense of superiority, my friends and I felt the last part not as a theory but as part of our daily lives. I felt it when I faced death in a urine-soaked hallway, staring at messengers with guns. I felt it when I took refuge in garages and dank basements filled with shit, knowing my life didn't matter. I slept on bricks for pillows, pillows that made my head hard and my heart harder.

I became a dealer.

I'd gotten caught up in what is known as "the drug culture"—but *culture* is the wrong word, or at least one meaning of it is. "Drug culture" suggests a collective effort to create something that lasts, a place where there are norms that are followed. But the drug culture I knew was more about solitude, not shared experience; and it was more about destruction, not a shared effort of creation. So I suppose *culture* is the right word in one sense—culture, as in an artificial medium in which things grow—in this case, pain and suffering.

By 1986, crack cocaine had overtaken Detroit. That was my childhood; it was the culture that shaped me. You could argue that crack hit Detroit worse than any other major American city, and I was primed to be a part of it.

Yet my first addiction was not to drugs but to the elusive hope of safety. We saw much older men, and sometimes women, getting rich and powerful on our dangerous streets, so of course we were drawn to the lifestyle. They, in turn, recognized a cheap labor force, one that wouldn't draw as much scrutiny by the police or punishment by the courts. These days, even in 2020, we hear horrifying stories of child soldiers—in Cameroon, Libya, Myanmar, Somalia, Sudan, Syria, Yemen—and the stories are heartbreaking. But in the drug culture in which I grew up, we were child soldiers, too. We didn't carry Kalashnikovs and we didn't march in formation and in uniform, but we were similarly brutalized and forced into violence and degradation by a world of adults who saw no difference between a child and a grown-up, whether those adults were the dealers or the police.

Eventually, I started using the drugs I was slinging. Crack was the shiny new object, the Mercedes-Benz of social party drugs. No one knew it was going to be so devastating. All we wanted was escape, escape from the shame we felt, and crack was the ultimate escape. ($30,000 worth of sales in one day? Hell, yeah, I'm not even a bit surprised.) I knew I was a smart kid—I wanted to be a doctor—but there I was, deep in the drug culture. I was doing shameful things, and the quick high of crack was too much to resist. I inhaled deeply of the drug and died momentarily as a thick plume of white smog pulled me into the darkness, the only place I felt safe.

But there was another price to pay. When they discovered that I'd been smoking the crack I was supposed to be selling, three grown men took me into a bathroom and pummeled me to mush. Heavy kicks bounced off my skull. There was no mercy in that world; everything was transactional. I was only as good as my last sale, and if I was smoking what I was supposed to be selling, I was a broken part of the machinery that needed to be bent back into shape. Eventually they gave up beating me, and as I lay on that bathroom floor, the coldness of the floor tiles was a great comfort; I remember resting my bloodied face there, listening to the footsteps recede. The blood pooled; my face grew cold; I was alone in pain and shame with no one to comfort me or kiss away the fear. In that terrifying moment, I cried razor blades, carving rivers of emptiness and sorrow in my young skin.

From that day on, pain became my traveling companion. I grew colder than the winds that blew across Lake Michigan, colder than the winds that froze Belle Isle, where we frolicked on the beach in warm weather.

That was my childhood.

I wasn't the first to cry the razor tears of addiction; I won't be the last. What of the addicted in our community—what of them?

Here, too, there's a cold reality: our addicted brothers and sisters are treated horribly. For women, their bodies become bargaining tools; their families lose trust in them; they're often brutalized on the streets. Men face physical assaults constantly. Their dignity disappears, and when they're arrested, they're often overcharged. We avoid any sense of empathy, because empathy is a danger we cannot afford. We are trying to keep our children away from it, so we can't allow ourselves to see the humanity of the addicted person; it's a threat too real to accommodate in our neighborhoods and homes. What this banishment does, of course, is pile shame upon shame upon shame for the addicted person. We may speak words that sound like empathy—that addiction is an illness, not a moral failing, for example—but we don't really mean them. We want the addicted person kept away in a kind of medieval hospital where the doors are locked and no one can get out. The addicted are given drug substitutes until those substitutes stop working; or else they're sent out into the streets when the money to treat them runs out, if there was any money in the first place; and they are too often nowhere near ready to return to the place where their shame forced them into addiction in the first place.

I knew that shame. When I left prison, I had spent the best part of two decades having every decision made for me. I had zero agency, zero whim or will, and then suddenly I was "free." At least that was how it looked to the world. In my head, I was still inside. I had a new addiction, one that mirrored the child's addiction to power and money. I committed to late nights, to partying, to women, to alcohol—the things I couldn't enjoy when I was inside. That was the PTSD and trauma of being free.

I was a boy-man trying to navigate adulthood, stuck in the mind of a nineteen-year-old kid who had never learned to moderate because everything had been decided for him in a brutal place—and now I was in my thirties with adult resources piled atop my lack of maturity. I carried with me a huge backpack filled with survivor's guilt—already, two of my nephews had been shot, and I still had a lot of friends in prison. These are the pressures our community faces. We feel guilty over our successes, knowing that our friends lie dead or in prison, the weight of our ancestors like burdens around our necks. Even when we're technically free, there are forces at work that keep us on a train line of pain: violence, imprisonment, poverty, racism. Even when we make something positive of it all, we're just a second away from being pulled over and having our records brought up on the little evil computer in a cop car. My forebears had gone through Hell and survived, all for me to end up in prison at nineteen for the murder of someone. How would I ever escape those burdens?

This, then, was the lethal mixture of pressure and shame I faced in the years after I left prison—or almost lethal, as you'll see.

What the cameras up above didn't see was me in my driveway that night, shaking, muttering to myself, "This has to change, this has to change."

I never drove drunk ever again; I gave that hurt boy trying to find his way . . . well, I gave him forgiveness from a place I didn't know I had.

Here's the stark truth about what it's like postprison in America: no one gives a fuck about you until it's time to hire you, rent you an apartment, or put cuffs on you for drunk driving. If you're hurting, this is the least significant part of your being. The culture will care about you insofar as it will use your past to deny you something; but it won't care if you admit that you're suffering.

So here's the only way out: your hurt and your pain and your healing and your happiness are your own responsibility. You have to choose how you want to navigate these things. Are these parts of your soul going to be eternally damaging and damning, or might they provide a moment of light through which you can grow? Because there is a deep power in recognizing your own fragility. When we have the courage to unearth the things that make us feel afraid, uncertain, or inadequate, it gives us the opportunity to strengthen those areas that would otherwise wreak havoc in our lives. The cracks in a structure widen until eventually they cause the building to collapse. It's better to find and fix the cracks than to have to rebuild from the ground up.

Every day, ask yourself this: What's the origin story of my life? You're the ultimate author of your life narrative, and remember this, too: when all about you feels lost and your imagination has run out of fuel, don't forget that no story stays the same for long. You have agency; you can decide to turn the page. You can sit in your driveway and decide to never drink and drive. (I still celebrate my life; I just take a car service instead of driving. I like shots of tequila, not entire bottles.) You can decide to advocate for your community. You can decide to be a better husband, boyfriend, father, or friend. Each moment of your life is the beginning of a new chapter in which you get to say, "This is how I choose to live."

There are four aged locks that sit on a table in our living room. They're small in dimension but enormous in meaning. Each lock symbolizes a different time in my life.

The small lock represents me locked up as a teenager. The lock next up in size represents me locked down in solitary. The third lock up in size represents me locked out of societal opportunities after my release from prison.

But the largest and most important lock represents me locked into my purpose. It's the biggest lock of all, because it represents the biggest leap of faith I had to take. It represents my understanding of how small the physically binding locks are in comparison to being locked into your authentic power, into your spiritual, intellectual, and emotional growth. It's the greatest freedom we can know. Those first three locks trapped my body, but they were incapable of trapping my mind. I am now a different kind of free.

The journey continues.

Yours,
Dad

Dear Jay, Dear Kalief

Dear Jay,

Someone asked me recently how I felt about going back into jails and prisons to do my work, and I remarked that what always hits me is the smell. It's an odor that never leaves you, and I've tried to work out exactly what it is. Is it the cheapest of cheap food slopped directly onto plastic trays? The putrid moldy bologna sandwiches and the nearly fermented orange juice and warm milk? Is it the body odor, a mixture of testosterone and fear? Is it desperation? Whatever it is that coats the very walls and floors and bars, I could be blindfolded, my hearing gone, but if you walked me into a prison, I would always know where I was from that stench. And that odor was never more vivid than on the day I went to Wayne County Jail to see you.

Nearly twenty years after my own arrest, I found myself walking back into that place. I didn't want to be there—God, I didn't—but I had to be. Beyond the smell, the sounds jarred me deep into my past:

keys jangling on the belts of the officers, doors slamming shut, distant shouts echoing down cell blocks.

At the desk, I found a middle-aged Black sheriff sitting like a statue, stern-faced, blank. Without a flicker of courtesy he took my ID, and I realized then that I'd have to report the visit to my parole officer—worse, I knew for certain that this guard was going to run my name through the system to see if I had any warrants, and it would surely bring up the fact that I had been recently released from prison. That was one of the many ridiculous things about being on parole: even in the midst of a private family matter, if I had any encounter with a law enforcement official, I had to report it to my agent. The thought of that tightened my throat, made the veins in my arms bulge.

After all those years on the inside, I was surprised to find myself so unnerved about being back, even as a visitor. Because I know these places brutalize; and sometimes this brutality is too much to bear. The thought of you in that place made me fearful of what might happen to you, and besides, you shouldn't have been there in the first place. You had been walking home from a night out, minding your own business, and you were picked up for nothing. Before you knew it, you were in handcuffs, thrown into the back of a squad car.

In my encounters with police as a teenager, it was clear that something in my life was terribly wrong, but no one ever asked me. I remember describing an incident to Oprah in an interview: how I'd gone home in fourth grade with a great report card, and my mother's reaction had been to throw a pan at me—it had missed and broken tiles on the wall behind me. Later, when Oprah asked when I'd left home, I said at fourteen, but she smartly pointed out that it had really happened that day when my efforts in school had been met with violence. It took her empathy and insight to make that connection; but out on the streets, young men like me and you were never afforded such an effort.

Kalief Browder was on his way back from a party when he and a friend were stopped by two New York City police officers. They arrested Kalief because someone said he'd stolen a backpack, but the complainant's story changed three times during the following weeks—first he said it had just happened, then two days previously, then, incredibly, two weeks earlier. The police didn't care to look into those discrepancies. I think that reaction comes from fear more than anything. Black communities terrify some police officers, especially when such communities are labeled "bad," and this becomes a self-fulfilling prophecy, a fear that leads to the abuse of due process or just a simple lack of good police work. Tragedies happen when members of law enforcement are afraid of the people they are supposed to be serving—what if I get stabbed or shot or get a disease? In Kalief's case, it was probably clear from the outset to the officers and the subsequent prosecutors that it was a lousy case, but still Kalief was arrested, his bail was set at $3,000, and his family could in no way afford the $900 that the bondsman would charge. So off he went to Rikers Island, at which point, a disaster was born.

If only we could train police officers to be more like nurses and doctors and less like soldiers . . . Clearly, they're still going to come up against people who want to hurt them— it's important to make sure that the public is safe—but they don't have to do so in a militarized way. If you're in the military, you start with the intention to kill, not to serve.

What's more, Black communities are often policed by white suburban men whose interpretation of that community comes from the news and the media. And the depiction in the media does not allow for a good Black father or a Black man who is not a criminal. Seldom do we see a boring, bland Black man living a boring, bland life—going to work, going to the store, cleaning out his gutters on the weekend. Oh, to see a Black man cleaning his fucking gutters on a weekend, hoping he's done in time to watch the Lions play. And because that's not what gets portrayed, it's no wonder that white officers driving into a city on a Monday morning, having spent their entire weekend cleaning gutters and puttering in peaceful suburbia, see only a hellscape where their lives are threatened at every turn.

It wasn't always this way. I grew up in a neighborhood where my early encounters with the police now seem as though they happened in a very different country.

One of the most obvious examples of this was a musical group called, amazingly, the Blue Pigs. That rock band, formed in 1970, was made up of police officers who would visit schools to play rock, soul, R&B, all with a message to get us to stay away from drugs. The group lasted nearly fifty years, and when I was a child, that's what the police were to us: they interacted with us, brought horses and helicopters to our schools so we could marvel at them—until later, when the helicopters hovered over us every night, as though we were in a war zone.

When the crack cocaine era hit, everything changed. Those

were the days when the police would just pull over in the hood and slam you up against the car. Even when cops gave us a break, it often came without due process. I was in my teens, selling drugs in a crack house, when the place was raided. By that point I was instinctively supersavvy—I dumped the drugs down the heat register, where they just burned up. The cops were whooping everyone's ass, and I remember this one officer saw me and shouted, "What the fuck are you doing in here?" I was fourteen, and he punched me in my balls, saying "Don't let me catch you here again." The officer took the money I had and drove me home to my father, which wasn't exactly justice, either.

We grew used to that shit happening because nobody ever saw it. But now everything, pretty much, is caught on cellphone, and still no justice arrives. Now people see it and you're *still* doing this shit and getting away with it?

In Kalief's case, he was held in custody for three years—three!—and eight hundred days of it were in solitary confinement. Kalief was not a gang member, but Rikers is one of the most dangerous places in America. He was placed in a Bloods house and had to look out for himself. Kalief's brother describes Rikers as "Gladiator School" (sadly, there are such gladiator schools all across the country where juveniles and adults are left to fight).

Kalief suffered beatings, both at the hands of the boys and the hands of corrections officers. The damage was done. In his time at Rikers, Kalief tried to commit suicide, as he himself put it, "five or six times." Meanwhile, his case was delayed and delayed, most likely because he kept refusing to take a plea. (He was innocent, after all.)

His story reminds me of yours, Jay. It was devastating to learn of your arrest and to know you had been picked up for being the first Black boy the police encountered. (They had been searching for armed robbery suspects in the neighborhood.) You were Kalief, and he was you; you were the Exonerated Five from Central Park, and they were you, and on and on and on, degradation piled upon degradation, injustice just the way of it.

There I was, though, that day in Wayne County Jail, wondering how you would be able to overcome this injustice. I thought, too, about what it would be like to go to my parole officer and tell him I'd been to see you. I could already see the smug look on his face. "Of course your son is in jail," he would say, "I mean, look who his dad is. You know that seventy percent of children with an incarcerated parent end up in prison, right? Chip off the old block."

Yes, I knew the statistics. I'd heard every assumption you could think of about the children of incarcerated parents going to prison. The old, evil saws: "I have seen three generations of men have a family reunion here" and "I met one kid who said he got himself arrested and sent to prison just to meet his dad."

For so long, Jay, we had defied the odds. I had made it out of prison without your coming in. As the guard handed me back my ID, I thought about my own father walking into that building to see me. What if this was the same officer who had processed my father all those years ago? How many fathers and sons had he witnessed living like this? How did he cope with seeing broken families at their lowest day after day after day? The coldness he displayed—was it his own fear writ large in ice? Was it disappointment? Was it resignation? Or, after all those years, had he just shut off his feelings as a way to save himself?

Before I could process all of that, I was taken to see you. On my way down the corridor, I thought about all the ways I'd tried to ensure that you didn't follow in my footsteps and all the ways I'd failed in that endeavor. Well, it was too late now. All I could do was prepare you to fight for your freedom and to prepare you mentally for prison, if things went as badly for you as they so often did for young Black men.

I fought back tears as I pictured you going through all the shit I had gone through. The degradation of being strip-searched; the constant threat of violence; food that would sicken, not nourish, your body; no access to a hug; no comfort of a loving family; not knowing who you can trust. Friends and family had been telling me for weeks that it was going to be okay, that Jay would be fine. I wanted to scream *I know you mean well, but none of you has served time.* No one is going to be all right in jail or prison. Everyone leaves there fucked up in some way. I thought about what had happened to me: How could I have been all right when so many family and friends were about to abandon me and move on with their lives as though I hadn't been born into this world? Imagine—friends you'd played basketball with; people you'd shared Thanksgivings and Christmases with; all gone, and for two decades.

The rest? They'd mean well, but what could they do? They were going to be so far out of your life, they could never imagine a place so cold, so dank, so terrifying. "It's going to be all right" hadn't been what I'd needed to hear, and it sure as shit wasn't what you'd need. So what could I say as I approached your cell and I dug into a deep, private space inside me, a kind of empty room where I rest when it feels as though everything is crumbling? What words could I find other than "It's going to be all right"? I'm a writer, but sometimes words feel so thin, like a kind of weak broth.

But we weren't quite repeating the cycle, because unlike me, you were innocent. The justice system tried to get you to plead guilty to a robbery you didn't commit.

I would find that out later in court, when the young DA came prancing in, ready to win whatever the cost. There was no sense of justice emanating from her that day as she pressed you to take a plea. This is a model that has worked for decades, to the point where the majority of Black men charged with crimes plead to lesser charges after prosecutors stack charges upon charges to intimidate them. What choice do they have? Already the system sees them as problems, as fearsome monsters. Why wouldn't someone plead to get less time in prison, when by not doing so they risk spending so many years behind bars? You were so afraid of her recommending a long sentence, Jay, that you almost gave her what she wanted. Fortunately, you held firm, but the fear in your face was that of a boy already jailed, already aware of the smells of prison, a smell impossible to staunch from the very DNA you carry.

You survived all of that. But I wonder what scars it has given you, deep scars that I may never see.

It's hard to maintain optimism. It's hard not to feel as though you're always up under this fucking weight of the past. How can I best help my son get through life, feeling empowered, feeling brave and confident, without his being damaged by all my shit? Staying in a perpetual state of anger certainly doesn't lead to solutions, that much I know. Instead, now I try always to ask myself, what is the solution? I think it's sharing authentic stories and telling authentic stories, no matter how devastating.

So it is with a heavy heart I must finish Kalief's story, at least as it pertains to his time on Earth. On June 6, 2015, two years after his release from Rikers, Kalief died by suicide. I believe that the trauma of what he'd been through haunted him and killed his imagination and his hope. I don't know how close I got to wanting to do the same, but I know I was close. I don't know how close you got, Jay, but I fear that anyone faced with a wrongful accusation will contemplate a cold world of ice just to be rid of it. But I do know that solitary confinement, false accusations, the rush to a plea deal, and the force of a police/judiciary that sees mass incarceration as the only tool for justice, all of it leads directly—in a straight line, provable, undeniable—to disasters like the death of Kalief Browder.

Talking to you now feels good in my spirit. You text me updates on what you're thinking about your life, and I don't automatically offer direction or advice. I've learned a lot these years. I'm no longer trying to be your mentor. I'm just being a dad. We appreciate the silence that comes over the phone, a silence we fill with what I think is love.

Jay, there's still a chance for us; we're both still here, both still alive. Our imaginations are still strong. What can we imagine out of all this? What brighter day might dawn if only we were able to talk, really talk, father and son?

Dad

Love Is Never Abuse

Dear Sekou,

I would like you to remain a child for as long as is possible. I would like you to be able to put off the concerns of adulthood—the pressures, the compromises, the disappointments—until your physical frame glows with the power of manhood. I would love not to have to write this letter to you, but I want you to be aware that your innocence faces a very specific threat, and I need you to be aware of it. Perhaps you can read this letter when you're a little older . . .

Growing up in the streets of Detroit, I learned very early on that being sexually active as a young boy is a thing that is celebrated. This goes beyond race. We tell boys that they should have as much sex as they want, that they're soft or weak if they're not sexually active, and that sex with older women is something to aspire to—it validates their manhood.

Perhaps the most famous case is that of Vili Fualaau and Mary Kay Letourneau. In the summer of

1996, thirteen-year-old Vili had sex with—no, was sexually assaulted by—his teacher, Mary Kay Letourneau.

When Vili was still just a sixth grader, they were already having sex. A child was born, and though Letourneau was convicted of two counts of second-degree child rape and sentenced to eighty-nine months in prison, she continued to see Vili after she got out on parole after three months and was reincarcerated for six years. Another daughter was born from the sex they'd had when she was out of prison. Once Letourneau was released for good, she and Vili married.

Vili had been open about the fact that he "went through a really dark time" while Letourneau was in prison, but in the press, the story morphed into something resembling a great romance. It was as if the world now accepted the love affair version of the story, not the abuse aspect. The two were married for fourteen years, separating in 2019. (Letourneau died of cancer in 2020.)

It's amazing to me that anyone ever thought that the relationship, probably the most famous child sex case in recent history, was ever anything other than a sexual assault case. Yes, they had children, and yes, they got married, but none of that takes away from the simple fact that he was thirteen years old when Letourneau sexually assaulted him.

The problem is widespread in our community, too, and it's time to become aware of it. Before we go any further, let me say this: it is not normal for a child to be exposed to sex, and it should not be celebrated. Black boys and men are seen as sexual beings; it is a viewpoint foisted on us without our consent, without thought, without any hope of denying it. So many of the terrible acts of violence against Black boys and men come from false allegations of sexual misconduct. What this means for you is that however you view your own sexuality, the mere color of your skin will dictate that you're seen as a sexual threat, a malevolent force.

But what about inside Black culture itself? Are we without blame? I'm afraid to tell you that we are not. Inside our own culture, young Black boys and men are sexualized; nonbinary, gay, and transgender people live under a constant threat of violence, all the way up to being killed. The power of this trope coming in from the white culture has permeated our own sense of self and left us confused and damaged.

Let me tell you about my experience. This is very hard for me to share, but I need to do so in order to warn you and educate you and hopefully steer you into a healthier, more complete, more fulfilling life.

I thought that being sexualized from an early age was normal. The messaging started early. I remember reading an article in a men's magazine when I was young and feeling confused when the men being interviewed talked about their child-hood sweethearts and their first memories of being in love. What was this love they were talking about? My experience had taught me that sex was not connected to the gentler feel-ings; it was purely transactional. I thought such talk meant that they were soft or square or both. As I read, I remember thinking that no one must have wanted them when they were younger, and that's why it had taken them so long to lose their virginity. Even then, they could only have sex once they felt love.

Whatever the reason, all I knew was that it was not my

experience, nor the experience of so many young Black boys and men around me. Deep down, though, I sensed something extraordinary, something I couldn't admit to myself: those men had made a conscious decision about when they wanted to become sexually active, a chance I'd never had. They talked about wanting to honor their sexuality, honor the experience of intimacy, honor their own bodies. And even though I sensed the beauty of it, it still felt like reading a foreign language.

My earliest sexual experiences were with older women. They were damaging and devastating. I will detail them here so that you can see how not to be, what to avoid. My hope is that you will learn from what happened to me.

My very first sexual encounter happened when I was around fourteen years old. Most people, if they're healthy and lucky, have their sexual experiences in a safe, private place, a place of intimacy and exploration not attached to the daily grind of life. Not so for me. Back then, I was fairly new to the crack cocaine trade and still painfully naive about the ways of the world.

One day I was selling crack for my brother out of a house on the east side of Detroit. I was part of a much older crew; the place was filled with older homies who knew so much more than I did about the dangers of life. That day, a woman came to the door offering to exchange oral sex for drugs. I was in the dining room, listening to the exchange, when my older homeboy called me over.

"Lil homie," he said, "she's going to suck your dick for a rock." There was no question about it. He stated it as a matter of fact, as if he were telling me it was sunny outside and the leaves on the trees were green. He had no idea if I'd ever been sexually active, and he didn't ask if I even wanted such an exchange. Among those men sex was not seen as a sacred thing, an act in which two people exchange love and cherish each other. It was part of a complicated and damaging bartering system, two bodies colliding against their deeper wills and needs. One, a boy; the other, a woman addicted; each preyed upon by those around them, preyed upon by each other, preyed upon by the culture in which they found themselves.

The actual act was terrifying, degrading, and sickening. I wasn't attracted to her. She was probably living on the streets, with all the physical degradation that brings down upon a human body, but I was too ashamed to say that I didn't want to do it. Yes, I wanted to be accepted by and fit in with the older guys in the crew. Yes, there was really no choice; they would have verbally brutalized me for saying no. But the truth of it was, I was a child. I had no way of processing the moment, no way of saying I didn't want to do it. I was not seen as the kid I was, just as the woman was not seen as a victim.

She was probably forty years old, the same age as our mothers, our aunts, perhaps some of our older sisters. Despite the fact that she was addicted, without shelter, and lost to the desperate streets of my hometown, she was also a person of authority because of her age. Yes, she was a customer, and this was commerce; I had a product she needed, and in the minds of the older guys, the transaction would benefit me. But behind it all, she was old enough to be my mother, my teacher, the pastor's wife. She held sway over me, even though I seemed to control the transaction.

Of course, I did not control the transaction; the older men did, and to them, it was nothing out of the ordinary. They weren't intending to wound the emotions of a young boy, set him up for abuse and pain. It was play to them. They thought they were doing me a solid.

Reluctantly I went to the side of the house, and she quickly unzipped my pants and went down on me. Quickly, I felt something I had never felt before—not pleasure or joy, just a physical sensation that overtook me, almost painful but powerful and secret in a way that engaged my deepest interest. Before long, she spat out my semen and gave me some encouraging words before sending me back into the house. I obeyed her; she had authority. Inside, my homie said, "She got some goodass head, don't she?" He said it nonchalantly again, as though discussing the weather. I nodded, then ran to the bathroom to clean myself up. Back in the dining room with the homies, I sat on the couch, my mind spinning—the addicting, euphoric ending had filled my blood with a kind of kinetic energy, an energy I knew I would need to foster and chase. But I also felt dirty, disgusted, and used.

I had been raped.

And then the floodgates opened.

A month or so later, I was seduced by another older woman. She was in her early twenties. Her words coiled off her thick, sensuous lips, and the warmth of her breath slid up my skin as she whispered, "I bet I can seduce you." She was not homeless; she was attractive. I didn't know what "seduce" meant, but when she pulled my hand toward her soft breasts, I knew that it was going to feel incredible.

That was where I felt confused. Something that felt wrong in my heart still felt right in my body; it was taboo, yes, but like many taboos, men in our community simply didn't talk about it.

The first time with her was at least less degrading than with the woman who was addicted. From that experience, my body became addicted to the warm pleasure she provided. It didn't matter that we were on a soiled mattress in the back room of a crack house or that she was an adult and I was a child. All I knew was that I felt as though I had died and gone to Heaven.

After our first sexual encounter, I couldn't stop thinking about her. Just one look at her sent a surge of excitement through my teenage body. I craved her even in the moments I knew I couldn't have her. My heart opened like a wildflower; eventually I convinced her to have sex with me a second time, but that time I found myself covered in her blood. I was terrified, as though I'd injured myself or her, and I had no idea what had happened until I got back to the bedroom and she said, "You made my period come down early, boy."

Those were my first encounters—devoid of intimacy, filled with things I could not understand, overwhelming, exciting, and yet degrading. They left me attracted to older women and addicted to meaningless and empty sex. For so many formative years, that was the only kind of sex I ever experienced.

In the following years I moved home to live with my father and stepmother. Part of me wanted to return to the innocence of childhood, but it was too late. I had been lured into the world of sex, and there was no turning back. I sought out sexually active girls and older women in the neighborhood, and sometimes they sought me out.

It is shocking to remember how many adult women I slept with when I was a young teenager. I sought out those older women, charmed them, and then lured them into taking advantage of my virility and youth. They knew the game, too; they allowed me to take control and dominate them as if I were a man capable of handling the complexities of such encounters. Then, just when I thought I had the game mastered, it turned, and women began to pursue me. They wanted what I could provide them—money or drugs—they never wanted me for me. I was a tool, a pawn in a seductive and twisted game. As long as I had drugs and money, I could have as many adult women as I desired. I slowly learned to set my emotions aside. If women could use me, hurt my feelings, and disregard my heart, it was only right that I do the same. It was that childlike logic that allowed me to disconnect my emotions and view women as nothing more than sex objects or things to be acquired.

But let's be clear once and for all: I was a child. Those were rapes.

Did I think of it as sexual assault then? No—I had no idea what was happening to me because the word "seduction" didn't sound violent or life threatening. It sounded alluring to my teenage ears. Something stirred in me that I had never felt before.

Sadly, those early sexual experiences, which occurred during the height of the crack epidemic, were not unique to me. Unhealthy sexual encounters between young drug dealers and women who would do anything for a hit were common. In my opinion, they were largely responsible for the misogyny that manifested in the music of that era. Let's not forget that most of the rappers of that time were young boys articulating what was happening in their communities. (People forget sometimes that those artists were just kids.)

Prior to crack entering our communities, it was nearly unheard of for women to be called "bitches" and "hoes," especially by boys. We had long been taught to respect and honor the women in our community. However, once crack took over and women began using their bodies as bartering tools, respect for them diminished. Can you imagine a fourteen-year-old boy trying to respect a woman whom at one time he had viewed with the same reverence he held for an aunt or mother but who was now aggressively pursuing him for sex in exchange for money, drugs, or prestige?

About nine years into my prison sentence, I began to examine my sexual experiences through a different lens. It was sickening to realize just how much pedophilia had been normalized in the world of my youth. As a teenage boy, the onus of responsibility had been on me, and I admit that I enjoyed many of the experiences. However, when I began to process all of this as an adult, I had a burning need to know why everyone around me thought it was okay for adult women to have sex with teenage boys, so I found someone to ask.

When I got out of prison, people from my old neighborhood began to send me friend requests on Facebook. I accepted all of them because I wanted to catch up with people, even the ones who had abandoned me. But eventually I started to delete those so-called friends because I didn't want to bring up old negative feelings.

While doing so, I came across a woman who used to live in my neighborhood. Her son and I were the same age and knew each other a bit. One summer, the woman had approached me pretty aggressively, and we had started to have sex, usually in her basement. Now, all these years later, the image of those encounters caused my stomach to turn. A sour taste filled my mouth as I remembered that adult woman having sex with the little boy I had been.

I could have walked away from those images, that taste in my mouth. Instead, I messaged her to ask what had happened to her to make it easy for her to have sex with me. She told me that she hadn't had a habit of having sex with young boys; basically, she had been drunk, and it had been out of character for her. In further conversations, she denied that she had had sex with another boy in the neighborhood, as I'd been told she had, and further, she claimed that the incident with me was well behind her—and totally forgotten about. Her conscience was "clean and clear."

This, then, is the depth of the problem. Even when confronted many years later, a perpetrator of abuse can put it down to alcohol or lessen its importance with claims of being morally good in the present day. (I won't bore you with the scripture she quoted at me.) She even asked if my attempts to understand what had happened to me and to hold her responsible were in some ways connected to my own shame about the murder I had committed.

Her messages to me were a harsh lesson in the way our culture still views Black boys as fair game, as somehow unharmed by abuse. Many of the men I grew up with had similar experiences, but very few called it rape. In our adolescent minds, we just thought we were being birthed into adulthood. But years later, when the novelty of reckless, empty, meaningless sex wore off, I realized how much we had all been violated. My innocence, such as it was, had been stripped from me, leaving in its wake nearly two decades of being incapable of loving or accepting love. Yes, I enjoyed the sex, but it came with a heavy price; my sexual and emotional health was compromised. I became promiscuous, sexually reckless, incapable of trusting women. I lost years that could never be replaced and was denied the pleasures and innocence of teenage love.

Yet the culture continues to reward such encounters and vilify the boys who suffer from them. It's the one culture I would love to see canceled and condemned. When I appeared on *The Breakfast Club* in 2017 and admitted that I'd been fourteen years old when an older woman had first raped me, a cohost, Charlamagne tha God, said he'd been just eight when it had happened to him. What was amazing about that interview was that when I said that I couldn't relate to girls of my own age because I'd been dealing with grown women, Charlamagne seemed to have an epiphany. He said, "I like older women, too—but I never looked at the correlation."

I know it is hard to look at women as sexual predators or to imagine them doing harm. In fact, I had so much fun sexually that it took a serious emotional leap for me to realize the extent of the damage those encounters caused.

Today I am proud to say that I am a survivor of rape, and I now have a healthy emotional outlook on women. But, Sekou, I don't ever want you to have to write the first half of the sentence I just wrote. I don't want you ever to think that honoring yourself, your partner, or your own body—or love—is something written in a language you cannot understand. This must be your language, innate and as uncomplicated as breathing.

Be proud of your body and honor it. Do not let anyone make you do anything you don't want to, and don't do harm to yourself. In all your dealings with love and sex, make honor your central quest. Cherish your lovers, cherish your own body, be considerate and respectful, and do not let the culture tell you that you are less than fully human. You are a Black boy. I celebrate that, in all its fullness and in the hope that you will one day live in a world that renders you not as an enslaved person, not as a chattel, not as a danger, but as a sweet, innocent, loved child, ready to move into adulthood and all its joys and challenges.

Dad

American Beauty

Dear Sekou,

Originally the castles were built to house gold, but that would not be the end of the story of the Gold Coast of Ghana. It was there that I finally began to understand the beauty of the Black experience—yes, there in the slave dungeons of western Africa.

Between the late fifteenth century until a full decade after the Declaration of Independence, the Portuguese oversaw the erection of hundreds of castle-forts along this coast. Gold and ivory were traded from them, and then the trade became more sinister. Eventually, the buildings were filled not with glistening metals but with people. They were held there in shackles until their captors pushed them through the door of no return, heading to the New World. They were our ancestors.

I traveled to Ghana in December 2019. On the way over, I was listening to rap and realized, with a great jolt, that the word "nigger" hadn't existed on the continent to which I was traveling. It was a word invented in the Americas, by Americans, to further denigrate and debase people who hadn't wanted to come in the first place.

I would never look at that word the same way again. Little did I know that it would be one of the many moments of clarity that trip would afford me.

The year 2019 was the four hundredth anniversary since the last slave ships had left and was slated to be a year of remembrance—the Year of Return. But I arrived two weeks before the festivities so that I could spend some private, intimate time there. There, on the Gold Coast, I read the worst three words I've ever read, hanging above the door to one of the hovels: "male slave dungeon."

I slipped through that door, down into the dank interior, where I stood upon the actual floor: a place where the blood, sweat, feces, urine, and tears of our ancestors had fossilized into a history so profane that I could barely breathe; yet I was also standing on four hundred years of survival. That DNA has persevered, has created a beauty no one can deny—it has created you, my son, and so many others, men and women who have contributed hundreds of years of progress to a country that does not cherish that sacrifice; yet we go on. Those floors bespeak the triumphant story of our enslaved ancestors, a triumph we can now birth into the world via our DNA.

Standing there in those dungeons I didn't feel only the sense of dread, the degradation, the obscenity of what had happened there; I felt, too, the pride of the men and women who had survived the passage, who had survived the horrors of slavery, who had fought against those horrors, and who had kept on fighting through Reconstruction and yet another migration and into the civil rights era and on to the streets of our cities today, now with bullhorns and masks and banners and a raised fist—*this* is our DNA, this is our skin. And within that skin, and despite my own missteps and sins, I have been able to produce magic in my work and fatherhood and mostly through nurturing you, my Sekou, the place in which the transcendent DNA of enslaved people finds its newest, most powerful, most potent expression, a boy filled with potential, who when he hears the date 1965, as you did yesterday in a casual conversation, as quick as a flash says, "The year of the Voting Rights Act."

This is what I think Nas meant when he talked about having the "blood of a slave/heart of a king."

All of that in you, a boy not yet nine years old.

Prior to my visit to the dungeons, I'd gone to Nsawam Prison. I couldn't have gone to Ghana and not paid my respects to my brothers and sisters who were incarcerated.

What I found amazed me. Despite the horrid conditions, there wasn't a mean spirit there—not even among the jailers. The poor conditions were due more to a lack of resources than to any meanness of spirit. I was accompanied on my visit by a woman named Femi Adetola. She pays for the women and men's medicine and food out of her own purse, and it's no exaggeration to say that she is an angel on Earth and one of my heroes.

What I didn't realize that day was that that visit was the perfect preparation for my subsequent visit to the slave dungeons. Black bodies in captivity—this is what they look like. I had lived it, but even I still needed reminding.

That was on my third day in Ghana; the next day I went to Osu Castle, which houses the slave dungeons. Right above the slave dungeons there's a quiet, white-walled church—small, with just a few pews and a giant crucifix on the wall above two simple chairs. I sat on a pew and found myself in tears as I contemplated the slave traders kneeling on the floor of this church, a floor that was also the ceiling of the dungeon below, where hundreds of souls awaited their terrible fate. You kneel down and pray in this house of worship, and right beneath you are the smell, the sounds of people suffering. They have no idea where they're headed. It's dark; there are feces everywhere. There is blood. There is the stench of terror.

How could you, you men above in that peaceful chapel? How could you pray? What were you praying for? And to whom? What kind of God wants such prayers?

I have been afforded the gift of being the person I was born to be, and so have you, my dear Sekou. Our skin and flesh are the very swagger of the earth; we are closer to the essence of life than any others. We feel its rhythms more powerfully, sing our planet's joys and woes more beautifully, contribute our blood and toil more fully than any. Think of what our culture has given to humanity, and in such circumstances! This is our magic, our ability to transcend darkness with a sure and confident gaze toward whatever light we might be able to discern. In four hundred years, we have grown from the wastelands of slavery to a mountainside, a high point where we can either keep climbing, or—no, there's no going back.

We're going to climb, you and me and all of us. We are going to stay fully present in our blackness amid the threats and accusations and suspicions; we are going to be the magic, and we are going to recognize the magic in one another, because when we do so . . . well, there's nothing more beautiful.

There's a rhythm in us that is so in tune with nature itself—it's in our walk, our dance, our creativity, our voice, our deepest selves. How can we not be filled with joy and appreciation when we recognize that? When you tap into who you are, it's immeasurable. How many of those ancestors could tap into their sense of pride and dignity and resilience and fortitude in such circumstances?

So many is the answer, because that pride and dignity are woven into our DNA. We can never outrun it, nor should we ever want to.

This pride and dignity are showing up in you every single day. I'm not just a proud father when I say that so many people recognize the uniqueness of your magical self. You attract so many people with your humor and kindness and smarts; the same can be said for Jay, too. This is the way of our community; we are called to reveal our magic despite, and inside of, a profoundly oppressive environment. There are so many opportunities for the narrative of pain to dominate our hearts, yet each day so many of us push away the lure of sorrow for a kind of manic joy, a creativity and kindness that are direct descendants of the broken souls of enslaved people. This choice is what sets us apart; we are forever choosing to recognize the magic of our own selves as a way of building a wall against the other narratives that dictate our place in society. That's the wizardry of our curiosity; that's the thing that speaks truth to us, even from our birth—a birth, lest we forget, into a world that wants to abort us before we're even conceived.

This choice to do magic, to be magical people, to let our curiosity and positivity shine? It's everywhere, if we only take the time to look. Yes, Sekou, there are men like LeBron James and Jay-Z and even Martin Luther King, Jr., and Malcolm X—great men all, but they're out of reach of our day-to-day reality. (This reminds me of something I once heard. When talking about prayer, a friend of mine once said, "Sometimes I just need a God with skin.") But I can offer you others to whom you can turn—these are just some of the heroes I'm gifting you, people who have taken the blood and tears of their ancestry and turned it into a healing water.

This truth is no better made flesh than in my friend Calvin Evans.

Calvin's difficult young life mirrored my own. Unlike me, he grew up in poverty, which was why he and his brother went to live with their grandmother in Detroit. She was working at GM and would come home coughing up fumes from the factory; Calvin couldn't bear that, and like me, when he looked around, the only people he saw making any money were the older men in the drug trade. So, like me, he got involved, mostly so his younger brothers wouldn't face the same life he had, and, like mine, his decisions ended in tragedy.

One day in September 1988, Calvin and a friend were going about their business in Mount Clemens, a small town northeast of Detroit near the shores of Anchor Bay. The two young men met a connection to buy crack, which they both could then sell. The deal went badly, and Calvin's friend shot the dealer, killing him.

Two years later, Calvin was convicted of the murder, a murder he had not committed, and given a long prison sentence. Calvin hadn't killed anyone, but the code of the street mandated that he not snitch on the guy who'd actually pulled the trigger.

We first met at the Michigan Reformatory—in solitary in 1993—then we were together in Adrian, Michigan. Years later we reconnected at Ojibway Correctional Facility, way up on the Michigan-Wisconsin border, a few miles from Lake Superior. I remember riding up there, seeing the beauty of northern Michigan as we crossed the Mackinaw Bridge. I was in the ugliest possible place—a prison bus—and as we crossed the bridge, I could sense the turmoil where Lakes Michigan and Huron swirled together below me. I marveled at the vast distances of water, as hopeful a vision as any human could get, and there was I, stuck on a bus, deep into my prison term but still able to resonate with the landscape. Perhaps being in that state of mind was why meeting Calvin became such a profound moment.

We first met without being able to see each other face-to-face. We were in solitary at the Michigan Reformatory in 1993, in one of the oldest cell blocks. I was on the bottom tier; Cal was on a tier above and a couple of cells over. Conversations went back and forth from cell to cell, tier to tier. Some guys would describe their old neighborhoods; some would sing. Sometimes a conversation between two men would become a conversation among many. I had heard Calvin debating passionately with a couple of guys about our responsibilities to our communities—with so much time to pass, guys were always debating things—and I felt instantly that he was someone I could connect with. I was still early in my development, reading a lot about Black revolutionaries, but Calvin and I were on the same page about contributing to the communities we'd helped destroy; we were big fans of books about Malcolm X and Marcus Garvey; and we loved all things sports. His presence swelled up into my heart like Lake Superior, immediately a friend and then a best friend. We ended up running into each other in various prisons in the North, and our friendship grew and grew.

Calvin is as funny as hell; he's silly in the best way. And perhaps because he's short and slight, he's very competitive. We were always getting into shit on the basketball court in prison because the bigger guys thought he couldn't play (and man, could he play). He had a jerky kind of jump shot that confused people, but more than that he was fearless and aggressive, and as we had both been in prison for so long, we'd developed a kind of swagger and reputation, especially on the basketball court. That swagger led to a ton of conflicts, but everyone, in the end, loved little Cal. And that's because everyone knew that he was the kind of person who'd give you the shirt off his back. In one interview he was quoted as saying "I just resigned myself to the idea that I would have to do this time, so I decided to be the best person I could be."

From the moment we met, I realized that Calvin was a person who served. He was constantly mentoring young men, gathering resources for those who had nothing, and giving words of encouragement to everyone he came across. He taught me so much about compassion—not compassion as some weakly, soft-focus thing but as a love born out of real conflict and trauma.

The perfect example was this: Calvin informed me that the guy who'd actually committed that murder all those years ago was now in prison with us, and the rule of the yard dictated that his unwillingness to take the blame for the death, thereby damning Calvin to more than two decades in prison for something he hadn't done, meant he'd have to be dealt with. That was the code by which we lived, and as I was a leader of the yard, the sanction for punishment of this man might well have to come from me. I was livid that that now-grown man had devastated Calvin's life, but Calvin was having none of it. "He was sixteen years old, Shaka," he said to me one day, realizing that the fate of the man was in my hands. "You need to protect him, not punish him. I'm counting on you to do that." That commitment to doing the right thing surpassed anything I could then imagine. To this day, I'm in awe of Calvin's ability to find the positive in people, to smile his way through pain, to be there for me when I needed him.

Toward the end of my sentence, I ran back into Calvin at Ojibway Correctional Facility in northern Michigan—almost as far from Detroit as you can be and still be in the state. It had been years since we'd seen each other; it was the first time he'd seen me since my longest stretch in solitary. Each day we would walk the track no matter how cold it was, and I'd tell him about my dreams of being a writer, a father, a man going back to society. It was so important then to create authentic friendships, and it remains one of the most crucial things men must do. My friendship with Calvin created a road map for the deep connections I enjoy today.

Everything came full circle when I was released a couple of years before Calvin was let out. One of the first places I went was to Calvin's mother's house, to fill her in on how he was doing. That was an immense privilege, but it didn't take long for me to realize why Calvin was such a great person. His mom made me the biggest breakfast I've ever seen and served it with love and compassion for this newly released man. I also got to meet his brother, Tap. As I ate that morning, I thought about the fact that when I'd been convicted, I'd been guilty of the crime. Imagine, then, the horror of being forced into such a dreadful, hopeless, and violent environment for something you didn't even do. I marveled at how Calvin had always been able to be fully present, serving the time as if he'd done the crime. And when he was finally released, I was proud to be able to help him navigate the shock of the outside world. Our friendship is now cemented deep into the earth, like the struts under the Mackinaw Bridge.

But there was a darker side to Calvin's acceptance of his fate. He had come to believe while he was incarcerated that because he had been involved in the drug trade, there were really only two outcomes he would've faced: a young death or a further spiral downward. Prison, for him, seemed like a second chance.

This is something that Calvin and I don't agree on, though I respect his feelings. Calvin reconciled himself to his condition by telling himself the story that prison saved him from that impending doom, as though those twenty-four years were justified by the life he had lived in the drug culture. I don't follow this line of reasoning. To me, if you're a Black boy growing up in a place where you already feel you're destined to die before you're twenty-one, there's lots of blame to go around before you start blaming yourself.

But I understand Calvin's position, too. Think for a second about Covid. When it hit, many in our community continued to party and hang out together, even though the virus was carving a terrible canyon through it. For people outside our dangerous street culture, it was the first time their mere existence had been threatened; but for many of us, the virus didn't seem as serious as an AK-47 bullet hitting us. Of the top ten things terrifying a young man in a tough neighborhood in America, I'm sorry to tell you that Covid doesn't even make it onto that list.

For Calvin, then, prison became a chance to escape the worst of his life and make a better one, and for that I and many others are eternally grateful. Calvin has gone on to mentor young Black men who've been victims of violence, using a technique called Trauma-Informed Care. (Put simply, this kind of care asks not "What's wrong with this person?" but "What happened to this person?").

Calvin now works to help young men navigate the aftershocks of the violence they've suffered. (How I wish I'd known him after I'd been shot as a young man.) He also helps with obtaining housing and getting appropriate treatment; and always, his humor and grace and intensity are rooted in the streets and prison. Even though he lost twenty-four years of his life, he always shows up as a gift to other people.

This, then, is your uncle Cal, Sekou—a man of great humor and dignity. Just don't think about rejecting his jump shot . . .

★   ★   ★

There are others who live out the DNA of the brave men and women of West Africa. All you have to do is look, and you'll find them.

One is Trabian Shorters.

Trabian started out as a leading tech entrepreneur, working his way up to the Knight Foundation, where he was the vice president of communities. At a conference in 1991 (coincidentally the same year I went to prison), a woman named Octavia Wilson challenged Trabian when he trotted out the idea that he'd had no good male role models in his life. This is often a truism of the Black community, that Black men are trouble, or when they're not trouble, they're just absent. This is a narrative forced upon us, and in many cases it's completely untrue: there are millions of great role models, and when that woman confronted Trabian, he realized that he'd had one of the best. His grandfather, Reverend Kennis Hutchons, Sr., had established a church, fed the hungry with a food pantry, refurbished houses, given jobs to people newly released from prison, and provided them transportation to and from work. Kennis Hutchons *was* a great role model, but Trabian had never publicly identified him as that. Fixated on the fact of his own father's incarceration, he had fallen back on the stereotype that there were no Black men of stature and inspiration.

With that realization, Trabian was (easily) able to start identifying the many Black men who were making a difference in their communities. In his book *Reach: 40 Black Men Speak on Living, Leading, and Succeeding,* he traced the ways in which this damaging narrative came to pass: with the onslaught of crack in our communities and the War on Drugs, Black men once again became demonized, both in white culture and to some extent within the Black community, too. We were the great threat, and we're still seen that way. That's why it's so easy for a police officer to shoot a young Black man running away; when you're seen as a threat, there's only one sure way to end that threat.

But it doesn't have to be that way, and it will take changing one person, one day at a time. Part of that new way of thinking has to come from within: from reframing the narrative we carry around inside and by committing to personal growth. As just one example, early on Trabian issued a challenge in Detroit and Philadelphia to identify great Black male role models from older guys on the block who fix bikes to barbershop owners who give free cuts to people applying for jobs to young men and women who cut the grass in the park so that kids can play there—well, he got more than three thousand entries in just those two cities. What that served to do, aside from identifying opportunities for investment, was to lift up good men and women, and show that Black men, especially, can transcend the culture's stereotypes and live out the full promise of their heritage.

From there, Trabian saw an opportunity to invest in communities financially. He eventually left the Knight Foundation to establish Black Male Engagement (BMe), an organization that invests in our communities. But the investment is not quite what you'd think; Trabian and his team don't wait for someone to show up with an organizational structure and a business plan. Instead, starting in eight different cities, BMe simply decided to invest in the men whose projects added benefit to a community—things like martial arts schools, bike repair shops, fashion and retail, even yoga classes led by Black men. BMe decided to honor what a community says about the applicant, rather than waiting on structures—fully formed nonprofits or fully fleshed out business plans—things that only slow up the process of change. Now BMe operates in cities all across the country, with more than thirty-five thousand community builders and more than three hundred Black male BMe leaders. Behind it all is Trabian's key question: "How do we create equitable outcomes for all members of our community?" The numbers are astonishing: the organization has received a full $4 million in grants already.

This is just one example of how the world is turning; slightly, slowly, but it's turning. Taken in hand with the changes in 2020, when so many people awoke to the injustices in our society, well, we should be hopeful; we can afford some hope.

When I think of hope, I think of Maurice Ashley. Sekou, you love to play chess, so it's wonderful to be able to point you to a role model who has made it to the very apex of that world. Maurice is the first Black chess grand master. He's a brilliant strategic thinker, and what's more, he's thought his way to the top. He hasn't written top-ten songs or broken any sports records, both of which I wish I could have done—or any of the other things our culture expects of Black men who are successful. No, he's used the power of his mind to break through in a completely different way.

And there are so many others, men and women you can always turn to for guidance, for support, and for inspiration. They were there for me when I was no one; they're still there for me as I move forward in my journey to inspire and change. I want you to think about their service, their commitment to change, and their love—as with so much else in these letters to you, their work comes down to love, always. It's the one thing that conquers all. I know this from dark experience; I have lived in a place with no love, and now I live in the love of these men and women.

One of the best you can turn to is Brittany Barnett, a corporate attorney who works pro bono on the side to get people out of prison. Her mother had been incarcerated, so she knew the price families paid, and eventually she created two nonprofits: the Buried Alive Project, which works to dismantle life-without-parole sentences, and Girls Embracing Mothers, which seeks to empower girls whose mothers are in prison. She also founded XVI Capital Partners and Milena Reign, both of which help formerly incarcerated people make their way in the world.

If you can't find Brittany, contact Susan Burton. She did six separate stints in jail but was able to break the cycle of addiction and incarceration and went on to create A New Way of Life Reentry Project, which works tirelessly to help women leaving prison create new lives. In the beginning, she simply went to the LA bus station and found women she could take into her home. It's no exaggeration to call her a modern-day Harriet Tubman for her work saving women who have led such difficult lives. Then there's Jessica Jackson from #cut50, who is now the chief advocacy officer for the Reform Alliance, an organization that works to end the abuse of probation and parole. Each of these women could have lost their career with the work they do—all it takes is one tragic story or an unpopular political stance to cause society to turn on organizations that work on the margins. But despite the risks, they have committed to serve the most vulnerable population, and their work saves lives every single day.

And there's always Scott Budnick—yeah, *that* Scott Budnick, the producer of the *Hangover* movies, who quit filmmaking for a while to create the Anti-Recidivism Coalition (ARC), thereby risking his career by working to free young people from prison. But the intersection of Scott's two worlds has changed lives from both sides. As he told the *Hollywood Reporter*, "Oftentimes, we have an A-list director . . . sitting on a couch with two people that just got out of prison that are looking for housing or jobs or going to college or a mentorship or therapy or whatever it may be. The conversations that happen on the couch in there are pretty great." Or else think about Sam Lewis, now the executive director of ARC. He spent twenty-four years in prison but now goes *back into* prisons to be a mentor. Imagine that, going back into such terrible places to change lives.

And then there's Van Jones. I could tell you so much about him, but here's one of the most poignant moments in our friendship. Remember when I told you earlier about not being able to get into the White House? Well, here's what happened inside that day: My not being able to get in caused Van to very carefully tear into the folks at the conference, saying they shouldn't be listening to him, they should be listening to me, and what a disgrace it was that I was barred from the building. Angie Martinez told me about it, and I watched a video of his address later—his voice was breaking; he looked so stricken, as though that was the greatest kind of insult. It was his chance to change policy and hearts and minds, and he did so by focusing on what was happening to me outside the building. This is love; this is compassion; this is Van.

You should look up to all these people. Most of all, you must internalize their successes, their struggles, their ability to overcome, and take that power forward with you in life. They are proof that we can overcome anything; that the blood and sweat and shit and tears of our African ancestors mean something. They're the essence of the magic of us—undeniable, physical, sacrosanct, profound, and beautiful. They have created an American beauty, of which you are the latest and most beautiful expression. To quote a T-shirt I once saw, "You are your ancestor's wildest dream." In fact, no ancestor could have dreamed the wonder of you.

Dad

Joy Day

Dear Sekou,

You were there, but I don't suppose you remember. You were just a baby in a stroller. Here's what happened:

Your "uncle" Fame has been an entrepreneur since he was fourteen years old—doing this, doing that, making this, making that. Eventually, he got into making T-shirts and was starting to create quite the buzz in Detroit. His empire would eventually stretch to three retail stores called Three Thirteen.

I met him when I was writing for a local newspaper called *The Michigan Citizen* a few months after I left prison. At the time he was building out his store in the heart of the northwest side of Detroit, and I quickly fell in with him. I liked his energy, his vibe, and he believed in me as a person, so we became partners. I opened a bookstore inside his shop and hustled every single book I could into the hands of an unsuspecting public. We were two poor

entrepreneurs. Our lunch every day was hot dogs that we
barbecued outside the shop on a little red grill.

One day Fame and I had a conversation about support-
ing the community. I thought it was important to provide
resources—everything from free food to free books—as part
of our business practices, but Fame didn't see how it would
generate revenue for either of us. He and I got into a real
debate about it. He was a businessman first and foremost,
and I was more of a social entrepreneur. Though Fame was
dedicated to the community, he was also a designer and artist, and oftentimes his focus was on creating the next great
look rather than organizing a food giveaway. But I believed
it wasn't enough to just ask the community to support us;
we needed to reciprocate if we wanted to create anything
meaningful.

It took convincing, but once Fame bought in, he was all
about it. We decided to put on what we called "Joy Day."
(We were on Joy Road, after all.) We figured we'd try to get
the whole community to come together to enjoy life for one
whole Saturday.

And off we went. We handed out flyers all over the neighborhood and then set out to solicit support from every store
on that stretch. We hit up the banks for a contribution (they
donated their parking lot), we got food and liquor from the
stores up and down the street, and we brought in face painters and made cupcakes. The kids were so excited—"Three
days to go!" they'd shout to us, then "Two more days!," then
"Tomorrow!" I decided to pass out as many books as I could
(I ended up giving away hundreds of books that day), and
we managed to feed four hundred people hot dogs and chips

while giving away a week's worth of groceries to two hundred families. We even remembered to tell the guys in the hood that whatever beefs they had needed to be put aside on Joy Day—and no drug deals, either. Everyone agreed.

The support of our community found its fullest expression that day from Cal and Tee, two barbers in the neighborhood. When Fame had asked them to participate, I hadn't been surprised when they'd told him they couldn't. Saturday was their busiest day, and Joy Day happened just before back to school. For men working on tips, a good Saturday made the difference between paying a bill and not paying a bill. It was a matter of survival for them; no one was getting rich cutting hair, so there were no hard feelings from Uncle Fame and me. Then suddenly, in the afternoon, without warning, a squad of barbers, all dressed in their capes and carrying their clippers, strode out of their shops onto Joy Road and proceeded to offer a free haircut to all the kids who couldn't afford one. Cal and Tee had seen the kids having fun and decided to close their shops, corral their staff, and head out to offer love and a number one all over.

Since that first Joy Day, Fame has lost his skepticism and gone on to become a key influencer of Detroit culture. He's opened his stores and kept them open in an unpopular place; and he's evolved into an incredible thought leader with a brand that people stand behind. But more than those accomplishments, he's taught me so many lessons about raising children. Fame is raising two kids as a single dad, all the while running his store. Watching the way his younger daughter was intimately involved in his business, I realized that I needed to share my work life with you so you could understand who I was becoming. I also learned how to balance work and father-hood and the importance of taking time out for myself when either of those things became overwhelming. Our friendship isn't the grunts and sports talk that many men share; it is deep, through tough times and good.

I hope you will remember this scene, Sekou: a bunch of barbers in their capes, striding like an army of love along Joy Road on the northwest side of Detroit—a place that had once thrived with music and cars but had now fallen into disrepair—all to give dignity and a fade to the children of Detroit. Those men are nameless now; their act of love is out there in the wind somewhere but rooted, too, in the commu-nity, in its sense of shared purpose and struggles overcome.

That was the essence of Joy Day: you ate chips, got your face painted, and eventually fell asleep amid the jangle of voices and laughter and full bellies and smart hairdos that day in Detroit. I hope the spirit of that day wheedled its way into your soul somehow. When you are older, you should create your own Joy Day somewhere (we had three of them, all told). When you do, I have every faith that the barbers of your city will step out from behind their chairs and spread the love, too.

Dad

To the Sons of Society

Dear Sekou and Jay,
You and I are going to create a different world together. It has already started, but this book is my commitment to you that you won't face what I faced.

We as a community need to change how we raise our boys. We have to let them cry—in fact, we must encourage it. We must be physically affectionate, we must listen, and we must wait on our reactions, not explode like rockets at the slightest thing. We need to create space in a world where a child's curiosity is nurtured, seen as an opportunity to learn the next biggest lesson or to create the next big thing.

One day I was browsing Facebook when I came upon a post that a friend, a poet named T. Miller, had written. Her nephew had just tested the water-proof capabilities of the new iPhone she had given him as a gift. The phone was ruined, even though it claimed to be waterproof. She was asking her followers what she should do.

Most of the comments encouraged her to punish

her nephew, but I wrote, "He was simply getting empirical data, as any scientist might." (Maybe Apple should hire him.) My comment reflects what I think we should do when it comes to Black kids in general and Black boys specifically: we have to give them the room to be curious without unduly punishing them for being children.

A few years ago, Sekou sat down next to me and asked if it was okay that he was drawing on his clothes with a Sharpie. He was beaming with pride as he continued to graffiti his expensive new jogging pants. "Sure," I said, "but you then gotta wear them." I took a video of Sekou and sent it to his mother, and we laughed about what would have happened to us if we'd been that bold as kids. If there was one thing I could change about the way we parent Black boys, it would be this: giving them permission to figure out the world.

Instead of this openness, Black children are too often being threatened with being "put out." If you can't abide by the rules of my house, they are told, you can get the fuck out. If you were a comedian and you did a bit about it in front of a Black audience, the crowd would be laughing and clapping, nodding to themselves that, yup, they heard that. These are our mothers, our grandmothers, our fathers, our grandfathers saying this. When I told Oprah about my childhood, she told me she'd heard the same. Whooping is so normal in the Black community. Oftentimes I'll get into a debate about it, and someone will make light of it. My answer is always the same: What would you do if your spouse came and woke you up in the middle of the night and whooped your ass with a belt for not doing the dishes?

See?

These are not rare stories in our community. That's why stand-up comedians make a living telling them in a funny way. But you, Sekou, will never face such a trauma; not at my hands, never. I will never traumatize your body—not just because it's wrong but because it sets up the normalization that this will happen to you as a Black man. Already, the Black body is not our own; it is controlled by the state, by corrections officers and police officers and all the other tools of oppressive society. Our culture has set us up to be inherently disconnected from our bodies.

In prison I was superresistant to strip searches, and I got into trouble a lot because of it—I often refused to spread because I refused to be dehumanized further. Eventually I had a conversation with an officer about it and realized how dehumanizing and degrading it is even for them. Imagine if your job for 40 hours a week was to look at assholes of various shades, various colors, shaved and unshaved. Eventually, after 160 hours a month of looking at assholes, you must surely become what you do.

Such are the horrors of my life. Imagine, then, the joy of you just randomly coming up and giving me a hug. Sometimes I need a hug, too, like the little boy I was never allowed to be. I think about when I was growing up in the hood and seeing young boys who never got hugs. Even in my own home, my dad wasn't a big hugger. It was something he had to navigate as a young father—he had joined the air force when he was around seventeen, so he had moved into a hard-nosed culture early on. His father hadn't been around much, either. Each year, though, his ability to show affection grew stronger, even when I was in prison. Through letters, he exhibited affection that landed just short of actual hugs. When I see my dad now, we immediately hug; my dream is for you both to be able to say the same for as long as I am alive.

This is what young boys are missing. I first noticed this in prison when I was teaching a class called "Houses of Healing." In that class, one of the most powerful moments was when the men would hug each other (they'd been sharing their traumas). Now I'm fortunate to see it every day with you—a hug can change a bad moment into something redemptive. Sekou, you fell over on your birthday and hurt yourself, but when we hugged it out, it calmed you, and the day was saved. Jay, when I came home after nineteen years, we hugged, and hugging you felt like hugging the little boy in me. There's a love that boys need from men that they can't get from their mothers. They need those hugs, they need their hair tousled, they need to sit at the feet of men who can share wisdom with them. That's what I want to create.

Men are as complex as women think they are. It's time we honored that, man to man, man to boy, boy to boy.

If you go through every possible way to die in America, we can tick every box: we lead on gun violence, suicide, cancer, heart disease—even Covid didn't let us slip in those evil rankings. This isn't to dismiss the trauma our society inflicts on Black women; it just explains why this cycle persists.

So we are left with little more than a survival mentality. You want to know why Black men work so hard and fight so hard and hit so hard in football, say? Why that intensity on every play? This is trauma. No, the defensive line on an NFL team is not generally playing with joy. It should be the pinnacle, making it to "the Big Dance." But this is survival, not joy.

This is what I want you never to know, this feeling that all you're doing is surviving, that your body is not your own, that you can't get love from the men in your life. I want you to flower, to expand, to taste every last drop of what the world has to offer. Yes, you will see overreactions, brutality, and the look on the face of white culture that may one day want to kill you because it's afraid of the imaginary ghost of who you can be. But you will have my love, Sekou, and the love of other men around you, and we will honor you, raise you up, and let you be fully human. This is the best we can do, and we will do our best every single day, word by word in this book, which I wrote for you and for all the sons of society.

In all these letters, I have tried to instill in you both a sense of wonder about the world, a hunger for love, not for violence, and permission to go and seek out the very best of our planet. We spin along upon it for such a brief time, and I don't want you to ever feel the burdens I felt, never know the fear I felt, the sense of dislocation. Black boys and men must forge a new path: one in which tears are cherished, love is paramount, and friendships are real and deep. Those in our community who struggle with addiction or abuse or neglect must be covered with healing hands, hands that you willingly reach out to all and any. I lost twenty years to a system that thought I was irredeemable; but somehow, through literature and letters and words, I was able to find a way out of the darkness into the light of this past decade.

I don't claim that it's been easy, nor that every day is a

dream. But my boys, my boys: when I think of your faces, hear your voices, and see your strong and beautiful bodies walk across this earth, I am reminded of the elemental perfection of nature, the magnitude of my good fortune, and the mere chance—one in billions—that I survived. That we came together for this fleeting span.

Isn't that enough? Let us make it enough, every second that we breathe this shared and magical air.

Dad

Acknowledgments

This book is inspired by my father, James C. White, whose letters during my nineteen-year incarceration comforted, inspired, and challenged me to evolve into the man I am today. I dedicate this book to the sons of society, including my two sons, Jay and Sekou.

I want to thank the following people who have played an integral role in my journey as a man, father, and leader. Without you all, none of what I have accomplished would have happened in the way it did. You have uplifted me, guided me, listened to me, and supported me because you all truly see me. For this I am thankful. Salute to the following dope people: Ben and Felicia Horowitz (family for life!), Reid Hoffman and Michelle Yee (true supporters from day one), Michelle Kydd Lee (my soul inspired sis), Oprah Winfrey, (my super agents) Cait Hoyt and Carisa Hays, Casie Cassanova (you are truly Clutch), Kayla Mason (your belief in me is first class), Adrienne Alexander (dopest lawyer ever), Erin Faulkner (thank you for being a sounding board for the proposal), Luke Dempsey (thank you for your light), Derek Reed (thankful for our second journey of words), Tina Constable (much respect Boss Lady), Melody Hobson, George Lucas, all my nieces and nephews, aunts and uncles, Indyego (Best Puppy Ever), Baratunde Thurston, Katie Mcgrath, and J. J. Abrams.

Salute to these Queens who always lift me while holding me down! Nana (you and the golden girls are the best), Tiffany Persons, Gayle King, Ava DuVernay, Maud Arnold, Chloe Arnold, Lashawn Peterson, Towana Peterson, Jessica Jackson, Topeka Sam, Tamica Neal, Vanessa Redd, Nakia White, Shamica White, Allahta Persons, Aaliyah Persons, Liz Dozier, Andrea Wishom (my sister in dopeness), Lakeisha Todd, Jess Sousa, and Niija Kuykendall.

A special thank-you to the men in my life who set the standard for fatherhood and manhood. Thank you for your wisdom and support over the years we have known one another. Calvin Evans, Clement "Fame" Brown, Jr., Ray Winans, Trenell Man Butler, Jerry Robinson, Trabian Shorters, Jason Wilson, Teferi Brent, Shawn Wilson, Dave Bing, Big Sean, Van Jones, Nas, Steve Stoute, Jerrel O'Neal, Jeff Johnson, Steve Pamon, Affion Crockett, Alan Maldanado, Darwin Filey, O'neil Brown, Mone Jones, Joi Ito, Colin Rainey, Sean Bonner, Scott Budnick, Sam Lewis, Alan Neal, Arthur Neal, Sherrod Redd, Will Redd, Lorenzo Persons, Elijuhel Persons, Bikila Ochoa, and Marlow "Slow Mo" White.

Thank you to all the organizations doing meaningful work in the world: MIT Directors Fellows, BMe Community, Prison Creative Arts Project, Men of Courage, Dream Corps,

#cut50, D Live, Good Time Boys, BOTS Reloaded, Anti-Recidivism Coalition, Hope and Redemption Team, Burton High School, Amity Foundation, Syncopated Ladies, Chicago Beyond, TripActions, Clubhouse, and COMMUNITYx.

To all my readers, I write for you.

One Love
Shaka

About the Author

Shaka Senghor is the head of Diversity, Equality & Inclusion at TripActions. He is also the president of Shaka Senghor, Inc. and the founder of Redeemed Sole.

Senghor is the author of the *New York Times* bestseller *Writing My Wrongs: Life, Death, and Redemption in an American Prison.*

Senghor is a former MIT Media Lab Director's Fellow and a former fellow in the inaugural class of the W. K. Kellogg Foundation's Community Leadership Network. His 2014 TED Talk was featured in their "Year in Ideas" roundup and has over 1.6 million views.

Senghor is the recipient of numerous awards, including the 2012 Black Male Engagement (BMe) Leadership Award, the 2015 Manchester University Innovator of the Year Award, the 2016 Ford Men of Courage Award, and the 2016 NAACP Great Expectations Award. He was recently recognized by OWN (the Oprah Winfrey Network) as a "Soul Igniter" in the inaugural class of the SuperSoul 100. He has taught at the University of Michigan and shares his story of redemption around the world.

Today, Senghor's priority is shifting societal narratives through storytelling and developing workshops with high entertainment value and deep social impact.

Senghor currently lives in Los Angeles with his younger son, Sekou, and their puppy, Indyego.

To inquire about booking Shaka Senghor for a speaking engagement, please contact the Penguin Random House Speakers Bureau at speakers@penguinrandomhouse.com.

About the Type

This book is set in Monotype Van Dijck. It is based on a type design attributed to the 17th-century German-born engraver and punchcutter Christoffel van Dijck, who became the most prominent type-founder of his time in the Netherlands. It is a graceful typeface, best used for setting books, quality magazines, and articles. Designed by Jan van Krimpen and released in 1935, it has two styles, Roman and Italic. The digital version was made by Robin Nicholas.